FROM THE PAGES

G000165882

The TROUBlE with OLD BOATS

ADRIAN MORGAN

ILLUSTRATIONS BY
CHARLOTTE WATTERS

FOREWORD BY
TOM CUNLIFFE

Adlard Coles Nautical
London

Contents

Published by Adlard Coles Nautical
an imprint of A & C Black Publishers Ltd
38 Soho Square, London W1D 3HB
www.adlardcoles.com

First edition 2008

ISBN 978-0-7136-8933-4

A CIP catalogue record for this book is available from the British Library.

This book is produced using paper that is made from wood grown in
managed, sustainable forests. It is natural, renewable and recyclable. The
logging and manufacturing processes conform to the environmental
regulations of the country of origin.

Typeset in 10 on 13pt La Gioconda
Printed and bound in Great Britain by Caligraving, Thetford, Norfolk

Foreword by Tom Cunliffe

The time once was when the career of a man was a pre-ordained straight line. The son of a sea pilot generally elected to follow his father. The children of a mill worker or a miner would have little choice but to do the same. A peer of the realm looked to his eldest to wear the coronet of destiny, and a gypsy boy took the long road of his ancestors to his life's end. Today, young folk outside the professions have little notion of an enduring calling, fully expecting to drift from one job to the unrelated next. Some rare free spirits, however, create their own vocations. One of these is to write about the sea.

Maritime writers are usually either newspaper journalists whose enthusiasm for the water drives them to make their passion their livelihood, or full-time sailors who discover a flair for the pen. Some are knowledgeable, some competent, some reliable, some even funny. A few write so well they could prosper in any literary milieu. One of these is Adrian Morgan. In his days as an independent contributor, editors could always look to him for a job demanding special tact, for a taut piece of reporting, or for a historic article that was as poetic as it was thoroughly researched. As an editor he had few equals, contriving to deliver what a magazine required without stifling the author's style or intent – a task demanding experience as well as talent.

So here we have a trained journalist who has become a specialist, sitting securely at the top of his profession. Suddenly, he decides to fly in the face of what fate seemed to have ordained for him, to quit the comparative security of his London life and follow a route where many have tried and failed. He gives it all up and becomes a wooden boatbuilder's apprentice. With the city flat sold, he moved to a croft on the West Coast of Scotland. Without false pride, he submitted to mastercraftsmen who knew futtocks, garboards and the benefits of red lead. He began as little more than a tea-boy, and slowly learned the skills needed to set up his own shop. In short, Adrian Morgan has had the courage to live the life many dream of but always find a sound reason to set aside.

Unlike many who re-invent themselves in middle years, Morgan is not the only beneficiary of his enterprise. Fortunately for the rest of us, the writer that was born inside him refuses to leave him alone, and he has recorded many of his impressions for *Classic Boat* magazine. Thus, all who read him can share his observations, his joys and his frustrations. They can learn, despair and rejoice with him all the way. But a smaller, steadily growing number are more richly rewarded. We have it on the best authority that these days he builds a very useful boat.

Introduction

These short pieces from *Classic Boat* have all appeared over the past ten years or so either as Sternposts or latterly as columns. They are in no chronological order, and thus the background will be confusing to all but my half dozen or so loyal readers, who will revel in the nostalgia and sense of *déjà vu*.

I came to wooden boat building late, but with the fervour of a converted smoker. Sadly, Ullapool Boat Builders, where I was taught to build clinker boats by Nat and Gill Wilson, Mark Stockl, Tim Loftus and Joe Hayes has gone the way of so many small boat building firms, crippled by overheads and dogged by the modern prejudice that 'wooden boats are just too much work'. I hope to prove that this is nonsense (and incidentally that plywood and epoxy are quite simply the Devil's Work).

Luckily, just as my career starts to wane, a new wave of young shipwrights is eschewing glass, resin and fibre for solid timber.

I've been lucky also to have had great editors: Bernard Hayman at *Yachting World*; Des Sleightholme ('JDS') at *Yachting Monthly*; Sir Peter Johnson, during my time as a book editor; and latterly Nic Compton and Dan Houston at *Classic Boat* where I washed up, prior to heading north via the *Scotsman* in Edinburgh to Ullapool, where I set up my own 'shop' (as the Americans would say) by the lochside as Viking Boats.

My thanks go to Rona who edited the typescript and put up with endless agonising over rabbet lines, scarphs, split ends and infinitives; to the late John Leather, who discouraged me; Tom Whitfield who keeps me straight, and of course, to Flo and Jo after whom I named my first commission, an 18ft Norwegian double ender, larch planked on steamed oak, called *Felicity John*.

1

Wood:
A Hopeless
Addiction

Wishful thoughts

An old copy of *Boats for Sale under £15,000* came into my hands the other day, so I ran a bath, stretched out under the patchouli bubbles (that's a giveaway) and settled down to an hour's wishful thinking. The classic content is minimal and the wooden contingent mostly rotten. However, amidst the glassfibre runabouts, launches, skiboats, ribs and rivercraft were a few gems, among them a 24ft (7.3m) Harrison Butler and a Cheoy Lee-built Vertue. The rest I wouldn't touch with a whisker pole.

But what tales lay behind the sale of so many boats, I wondered; of bank balances overdrawn and wives who hated the sea; of too little time and too far to go; and wet weekends spent listening to the wind. Of projects abandoned – including one particularly sad-looking steel cruising boat, all slab sides and ugly coachroof: 'The boat comes with welding gear and enough steel to complete,' ran the ad. '£15,000 ono.' I'd offer £1,800 cash and bet the fellow'd bite your hand off...

Such a huge collection of, mostly, unsuitable and ugly-looking boats left me depressed. All the boats I've ever owned were cherished and passed on with regrets and a hatful of memories. From a close reading between the lines of their impossibly optimistic descriptions, most of these were clearly on the market through desperation and broken dreams.

Saddest of all, cheek by jowl with all that redundant glassfibre were also a number of run-of-the-mill wooden boats, coming to the end of their lives, survivors from the 1950s, the words underneath the pictures – taken from the most flattering side, like faded starlets – speaking of 'some remedial work' or the euphemistic 'needs some attention'. The clinker river boat, ship's lifeboat, naval barge, workboat, narrowboat lined up like hopeless mutts awaiting rescue at the Battersea Dogs' Home.

Then again, maybe not so hopeless. Take the Jaguar 23 outside my shed as I write. It's a wonder what can be done with even the leakiest basket case, given enough time and elbow grease. The January storm threw it off its trailer, ripping off the bilge keels. I can't say I warmed to it, but it was work. Then, after a few days, all that began to change. I began to see beyond the appallingly shoddy workmanship, the almost complete lack of integrity in her build. Somewhere in there was a not-bad looking boat, struggling to get out. And once the keels had been fixed back on, the pathetic washers and feeble bolts that had failed to keep them connected with the hull replaced by hefty plywood backing pads, the interior wood-work oiled and the topsides given a wax and polish the 'it' became a she. I almost fancied having a spin in her. Probably not a bad little mover.

But all things are relative; sow's ears do not ever – despite wax polish and stainless steel washers – silk purses make. A Jaguar's a Jaguar's a Jaguar;

never a classic. Just one of thousands of boats popped out for a greedy public in the 1970s, slapped together by kids in overalls with brushes and buckets of goo. Not like – and you'll know what's coming next – not like a proper, wooden boat. A proper boat such as *Maureen*, which you see here in the drawing by her co-owner Charlotte Watters, propped up against the stone pier at Ardmair near Ullapool.

Built by Percy See of Fareham in the mid-1920s, she is a far cry from that Jaguar. *Maureen* was built by people with real skills, who cared, and her new owners all these years later still care, or they would not have spent every other weekend for a year stripping her out, reframing her, canvassing the decks, dropping the keel and tackling a hundred other tasks that old wooden boats require once they've passed a certain age. The same storm that ripped off the Jaguar's keels nearly wrecked *Maureen*. But there was never any question of giving up on her.

Not all wooden boats are worth saving, of course, but we all know – or we would be reading *Boats for Sale* – that it's somehow more rewarding to restore boats properly built in wood. And for the life of me I cannot think why that should be. Something to do, not with the material, but the integrity with which they were built, perhaps?

Go north young man

Answer me this. Why were only two boats under sail on the wide Solent the other weekend, the sunny one after those interminable weeks of gloom? And why was it that they had a combined age of over 130 years?

Aha. Must be the extreme hardiness of old wooden boat owners, you say. It could be that rare sense of adventure that goes with ownership of old wooden boats.

Could be none of these things. My guess is that it's because, perforce, wooden boats are best left in the water, open to temptation, even when the cold winds of winter blow. The more cynical might go further, arguing that it was because wooden boat owners spend so much time fettling while fair summers' winds blow to waste that they must make the most of every scrap of good weather, even if it falls in early January when only the fool-hardy (and the cheap-rate Yachtmaster students) venture afloat.

Thus it was, against a backdrop of lines of overwintering, shored up glassfibre, the two old girls slipped down river and found themselves in Newtown, then crept up against the dying ebb to Buckler's Hard as they have so many times before. And, apart from the chill in the air, it might have been early spring, not the back end of a winter that has proved every bit as cantankerous as the summer.

That weekend, when the ice formed overnight on the deck and the morning air was as clear as a cut-glass decanter, was the best sailing for months. February is usually gloomy no matter how many times you tell yourself the days are getting longer. And come spring the old girl could be heading up north to Scotland, so there was a poignancy in the sailing. It could be her last Solent outing for a while.

It'll be entirely up to her, of course. After 65 years or so she has, if not a mind of her own, a way of influencing her current owner's. Could be she intends to settle down south for good, and if so my plans will prove academic.

If she does co-operate, how best to get her there has been exercising my mind. North Sea or Irish Sea? That is the question.

Clearly Scotland's west coast offers the more attractive cruising grounds. A long dawdle down to the West Country, old haunts, round the corner and up the Irish Sea. Maybe a stopover in the Republic. A Guinness or three, a night of wild Celtic fiddle playing, then hoist the hangover aboard and head for the Clyde.

Or maybe the east coast. Quicker. Hook into a south-westerly and go for it non stop, reaching the Forth in a few days. Plenty of cruising for a season at least between South Queensferry and North Berwick, then around the top, or through the Caledonian Canal, and explore the west coast next year.

Either way it would be an adventure. Did not Humphrey Barton, mid-wife to the Vertue class, and facing the same dilemma, hesitate at the mouth of the Lymington river and agonise 'left or right?' before delivering *Monie*, V3, anticlockwise round Britain to her new owner in Wales? Ducking the obvious question 'did he really have charts and tidal atlases for both routes?', what would 'Hum' himself have advised a vastly less experienced owner in V2?

Lacking the gift of communication with the dead, I was fortunate to find myself at a tableful of Yachtmasters the other day. Who better to advise on whether to go east or westabout. The rigours of the North Sea, or the dangers of the Irish? They were all the same to me.

After a deal of frowns, exchanged glances and toying of beer glasses (but no discussion) a silent consensus was reached: 'Adrian, old chap. We are of like mind. There can be no doubt of the matter,' says the spokes-man, whom we shall call Tom, stroking his chin. 'No disrespect, but we strongly advise you to take the old girl up by road.' Now what am I supposed to make of that?

Simplicate, its simpler

Simplicate and add lightness. It was a Herreshoff, Nathanael, perhaps, or L Frances who coined the phrase many years ago but the sentiment has always been relevant to the building of yachts. 'Weight is only good in a steamroller,' was Uffa Fox's take on it. And as I begin to contemplate buil-ding my first ever mast, the subject of strength versus weight is beginning to occupy my thoughts.

Just as any fool can be cold and wet on a boat, any idiot can build a mast that won't fall down. Without being too rude about some of the gaff- and lug-rigged boats seen at classic shows, many of them could do with a dose of Uffa and Nat's advice. It seems that, in the quest for rugged authenticity we may have thrown out some of the structural engineering lessons so painfully learnt over the years.

Listen to this, from *Yachting Monthly*, August 1929 in a report on the 14ft (4.3m) International Class: 'The mast of the Morgan Giles boat is remarkable for its small diameter and lightness to compensate for the lighter plate carried' and 'The masts in the Fox boats may be described as hollow planks streamlined at the after edge and with a luff rope of the sail in a groove...' Clearly both designers had gone to great lengths in perfectly matching mast to boat; the former being U-sectioned, the latter more V-ed and carrying a centreplate 'of considerable weight'.

My safest option is to build heavy. But is it? Weight puts undue strain on the structure and needs heavier standing rigging and fittings. Weight aloft must be balanced by ballast below and, if my maths are correct, a pound of lead 20ft (6m) aloft is equal to 4lb at 5ft (1.5m) or so below the waterline (though the designers among you will be quick to correct me). Clearly then weight aloft is bad news, unless you are aiming for an easy motion. I am aiming for speed and without squandering any of the righting force exerted by the centreboard.

Thing is this 18-footer (5.5m), designed by one Karsten Ausland in 1934, was built by a man who worked for Nevins yard in New York, which wrote the rule book for boat construction. That means I have a great deal to live up to. It would be easy to slap a great tree trunk on top of her, but that would ruin performance and turn this sea bird into a dodo. If Uffa and Morgan could do it in 1934, then surely another Morgan in 2002 should be able to achieve something similar? It will certainly be a challenge, and one that will involve spruce – if we can get the right quality at the right price – and much hollowing (and cursing).

The old phrase 'simplicate and add lightness' came again to mind recently with the death of Bernard Hayman, former editor of *Yachting World*. It formed the basis of one of his editorials during my time with the magazine. He had been very much taken with the Frances 26 designed by Chuck Paine. The early version was flush decked and gloriously simple. No standing headroom, but then Bernard would say 'what's the use of headroom in a twenty-six-footer? You go below, you sit down, you sleep.' It echoes Uffa Fox: 'Headroom's only useful in a caravan.' And below a certain length, headroom is just not feasible in a boat without ruining her lines.

Bernard, who was to buy a Frances 26 hull and have her fitted out to his satisfaction, was a voice, as usual, crying in the wilderness. The Frances by popular demand soon sprouted a lid, and her looks were indeed ruined in the cause of headroom. The simplicity that was so appealing was lost.

As I come to build my mast and fit out *Jan*, Ausland's lovely double-ended camping cruiser, Bernard, Uffa, Morgan and even the ghost of old Nat will be looking over my shoulder, wincing no doubt at times, always encouraging me not to forsake the principles they believed in and fought so hard for. I cannot hope to match the dinghy building brilliance of Mssrs Fox and Giles – the paper-thin planking and myriad tiny ribs – and the genius of Herreshoff is way beyond me. I will, however, keep my old editor in mind. Always logical, always forthright it was he, on my asking what he thought of the new boat with which I had fallen in love, who replied 'Hm. Boom's much too low'. And he was right. It took me a crack on the head to heed his advice and raise it, however.

Bloody weather

Spring finally sprung into the Highlands in mid-May, lingered for two days and departed as swiftly, leaving a dusting of snow and a sense of déjà vu – just enough time to scrape the cappings, varnish the cockpit, paint the decks, refurbish the cockpit and turn the rusty Yanmar into a thing of shining, silvery beauty.

So seductive was the weather, so apparently settled (although, from experience, so fleeting the window of opportunity) that I wasted no time, camping aboard *Sally* for the night amid the wreckage of dismantled galley furniture, paint tins and tools. It brought back memories of the time I fitted the engine, way back in 1997. Then it was midwinter and, with no bridgedeck to keep out the snow, had it not been for the hot air gun pressed into service as a space heater I would surely have frozen to death. It was, as they say, a bonding experience.

This time around there was no need for a makeshift heater; and as the sun set behind the Summer Isles I raised a glass of gin and tonic (salvaged from the bilges), fired up a tin of baked beans and some corned beef (lurking in a locker) on the dregs of last year's butane, ate them straight from the frying pan, then snuggled into my sleeping bag as the sun faded, and fell asleep to Radio 3.

Early morning saw me scratching back the first coat of varnish and slapping on a second, before breakfasting on what remained of the beef and beans, washed down with the dregs of last year's coffee grounds. That left just a tin of tuna and a can of chopped tomatoes for lunch. True luxury.

By midday the varnish was drying and a start made on the foredeck. An RAF fighter dipped low over Loggie Bay. Here on *Sally*, back in 1937, or up there in 2005, dodging the mountains, at just under Mach 1, where would I rather be? No question.

By early afternoon the cockpit was varnished and primer was drying on the coachroof sides. Lunch had slipped down like a meal at the Ritz and all seemed well with the world. Then it began to feel moist; a haze began to envelop the sun. Soon the moistness had become dampness, and soon after that, wetness. The surface of the water became pock marked with droplets. For some moments I was in denial. This could not be happening. Winter had reappeared.

'Bloody weather,' I yelled, to the astonishment of a fellow in a kilt walking his dog by the shore, as my still soft varnish work began to take a beating.

Then Stuart swings by in his tender. Now Stuart is a philosophical sort of chap, used to the vicissitudes of Highland weather, the uncertainties of sun and rain. He takes one look at my rain speckled brightwork, shrugs and with a wry smile says, 'Nice, non-slip Highland finish you've got there.'

Yup, gone for good are the days of high gloss Solent finishes. Of yacht quality topsides and Bristol fashion. That afternoon *Sally* ceased being a pampered southerner. From now on it'll be pot luck if she begins the season looking immaculate or just well protected. Perfection will have to wait a while longer. I'll just have to settle for a fine fishing boat finish, or even just an honest fishing boat finish.

The value of vessels

Vessels have been on my mind recently. To be more specific, boats and pots. Which has been of most value to mankind over the millennia?

An odd question, you may ask, and probably brought on by a pottery course I have just embarked upon and the end of my time at the yard, learning the essential skills of a boatbuilder up here in the wild north-west of Scotland.

How then shall we argue the case? Without pots ancient man could not heat food over burning embers. Ah yes, but without boats he would not have been able to find the food or transport the pots when man became a trader. Besides, you can tear a piece of meat, roasted over an open fire, with your bare hands, but only one man could walk on water (and he was a carpenter). Pots, schpots. You need a boat.

I played the pots versus boats game with myself for hours before concluding, what the hell? If you're a potter you value pots; if a boatbuilder then boats are the be-all-and-end-all of human endeavour. This would seem to be borne out by the respect in which medieval shipwrights were held. You only have to look at the accommodation offered by the Montagues to their master builder next time you're at Buckler's Hard. You'll note they put him up in a four star hotel with nice views overlooking the Beaulieu river. Nowhere do you see a sign saying Master Potter's House. Unless it's that hovel, second right after the blockmaker's apprentice.

The potter and boatbuilder are linked, of course, albeit by similar but opposite aims; one strives to keep water out, the other is keen to make sure the liquid remains within. Both use their hands in a way that produces curvaceous forms that grow organically. And at the highest level of skill they are among the finest of craftsmen. A good potter can hold his head up among a crowd of average boatbuilders.

Then it all goes awry. A pot by a Japanese master will fetch hundreds of thousands of pounds. Not so a boat, even by a master such as Uffa Fox, Morgan Giles of Fife. An International 14, which may have taken Uffa many weeks to build using the finest materials, woven together in an intricate matrix – a race winner from the 1930s – will only change hands for a few hundred. Old Fireflies are two a penny.

Nothing new here, you say. The old art versus craft argument. Boatbuilders will always be just craftsmen, hence what they make will always be less valuable than anything constructed by an artist. We may hear that 'old Fife was an artist' but even after his death a gorgeous 6 Metre will attract more chopped in half neatly down the centre line and pickled in brine à la Damien Hirst or filled with concrete, like a Rachel Whiteread sculpture (or burnt as a piece of performance theatre?).

We see old boats used as furniture. Guy Fawkes Night tinder. A German came into the yard last year looking for a clinker hull. 'It vill be around two metres thirty', he said. To scull across Lake Constance? As a tender to his Folkboat? 'Nein as a, how do you say, book case?' Yup, wanted it to keep his old copies of *Boot* magazine.

Meanwhile councils consign old fishing boats to parks, filled with spring-flowering bulbs. (In Oman there's a beautifully kept dhow on a roundabout).

So what's all this about? That we don't value our master boatbuilders as we do our master potters? That boatbuilding should be classed as an art, not a craft? That we should try building boats out of clay? If it were possible they'd have tried it centuries ago, wouldn't they? For potters and boatbuilders are nothing if not ingenious. Yet given the longevity of pottery and its ability to take hard knocks, a clay boat doesn't seem so far fetched. Certainly that hideous mug I made at school 30 years ago has never leaked and defies all my mother's attempts to destroy it. Now all I need is enough clay and a potter with an oven big enough to fire a 20-footer.

The power of words

Occasionally words come back to haunt you, although in my case I have to say, very seldom. I write, you read – at least I'd like to think some of you do – and then silence. It's disheartening. Unless there's a mistake, such as the time I suggested the *Titanic* was built on the Clyde, or that the *Queen Mary's* lifeboats were clinker built. Or, or…

So what's this about the power of the written word? The ability to move people? Obviously not my written words.

Yet there was one time when something I wrote did have a profound effect, albeit not of a world-shattering kind. And I only discovered years later when the man whose world had been shattered took me aside.

'It was you, then,' he said. 'You're responsible for persuading me to buy that old Folkboat.'

It had been one of those hectic, deadline-induced paragraphs, slotted in to fill a few column inches in the Getting Afloat section of *Classic Boat*. At the time I'd been on something of a crusade to point out how cheaply you could get afloat in something old and wooden. We'd trawled the small ads for '2 1/2 tonner in need of TLC. £1,200 to a good owner…' type of boats. 'Goodness gracious,' I said (we only used classic expletives at *Classic Boat*). 'Do you realise that, for the cost of antifouling your Beneteau you could buy an example of one of the finest little boats ever produced?'

Having been similarly smitten in my time by a 1937 5-tonner going for, what seemed, a ridiculous price I was evangelic in my desire to pass on the truth about old wooden boats. They were stupidly under priced. And the joy of sailing them was only eclipsed by the pleasure of maintaining them. In my view.

Thus it was that my eye had fallen on this Folkboat. It may have been £500, perhaps a little more. The description sounded promising, or perhaps I should say not terminal. 'Some damage to planking… sails new in 1964 and hardly used. Echo sounder, and many spares…' You know the kind of thing. And indeed the photo, taken not surprisingly from her good side, looked promising.

Given the deadline I didn't phone the seller. He'd only tell me half-truths. I could see what I needed, so I wrote something to the effect:

'Now here's a project for a keen young man. Built in 1964 of mahogany on oak she deserves a few more years afloat. She's basically sound, carries a suit of decent sails and with a few quid spent would more than reward her owner. She's lying ashore, having sustained some damage which her owner says is "eminently fixable". He's eager to pass her on to a loving owner, one who will cherish her into her old age and derive pleasure from a boat that is surely a classic among classics...'

And thus I set in motion an unstoppable process, fuelled by romanticism, fed by nostalgia.

It so happened that my words were read by a young man. Inspired, he made the pilgrimage to that boatyard where he found her in a corner, propped up against a shed. Her undamaged side did indeed look fine and the rest – well he could fix that, no problem. Enthusiasm and youth are wonderful things.

Fast forward a couple of years. The boat in question is now on the north-west coast. She's been sheathed in Cascover. But still she leaks. Her owner has lost that rosy glow, and yet he's still besotted. Well, at any rate, he's stuck with her now. She's taken every spare penny he has and every spare minute. For that he could have bought something halfway decent. But he's had some grand times in her, between pumps. She's taken him and his bride on honeymoon to St Kilda for a start, and virtually the length of Scotland's west coast. They've come through gales and calms (once he rowed her for ten miles). Did I say she had no engine?

And today she's still afloat. Sheathing stripped off, refastened, new frames, recaulked, fresh paint, and leak-free. Last season they took her to the Faroes. This year they plan to cruise Skye and the Outer Isles.

'So you were the one who wrote that piece in *Classic Boat*. I suppose I'd have to thank you.' There must have been times when he'd wanted to curse me.

Curiouser and curiouser

Oh, clinker can be so cruel; showing up every tiny defect of line. The eye will pick up the merest hint of unfairness in the run of planking. Not a millimetre will go unnoticed, and it's no good anyone telling you it will.

It's all down to eye. You mark off the line of planks on the moulds, and keep to them, then at some point your eye will tell you to move them. Why is still a mystery to me. Four clinker boats to my name and some of the mysteries of planking leave me scratching my head.

For instance, take the third plank up on my fourth boat. Spiled as carefully as I could. Checked and checked again. Spile board shuggled around until entirely satisfied. Bow and stern clearly marked. Moulds too. Board cut and planed. Thicknessed. Plank fitted.

Plank fitted? You're joking. Plank most certainly would not fit. As it rose from the flattish midships section to meet the sternpost it was clearly in need of more pressure than was healthy to persuade it to join its lower neighbour.

So it was plank off and checked against the spile board. Perfect. Little prayer. Back on, and would it go? Would it hell.

As this was an uncommonly fine piece of Black Isle larch, knotless and noble, and aware of the wastage that goes with wooden boatbuilding, I was loathe to cast it (and its mirror-image opposite) aside and start over. Nevertheless, after the fourth attempt to torture the poor board into place I gave up, lit a fag – something I reserve for rare occasions – brewed up and thought a bit. Perhaps I'd got it the wrong way round, spiled to the wrong edge? Nope. So I clamped the spile board back onto the last plank. Nope. Matched fine.

Finally, rather in desperation, I took the ill-fitting plank off, flipped it bow to stern, and, well whadayaknow? Perfect fit right down the line. Land width a constant $3/4$ in from stem to stern. A complete mystery. And if anyone has an explanation, I'd be happy to hear from them.

I'd be happy also to hear from anyone about some of the other unfathomables. Who, for instance, can explain how a plank that takes a huge dive at the stern, when roved up looks as fair as a fair thing? Or where my 12mm chisel went when I wanted it most and why it turned up when I didn't? Suppose they're just more of those biblical ways of a ship in the sea; ways of a man with a maid kind of things. Unfathomable.

Then again, what do I know after four boats? After a score, perhaps. Some boatbuilders can skin up a dinghy without moulds just by eye. There's one such over in Skye. Malcolm says they get in the way. I can't see how, if you're trying to build to a designer's plans, you can do away with moulds – unless you've built hundreds. Which means it's 96 to go before I can say 'ah, when you've built as many as I have'. By which time I'll be smoking a pipe, which will add immeasurably to the authority in those words.

As for authority, who knew the late Davey Elliott from the Elephant on the Hamble? Just a whiff of his Old Navy Cut down the breeze was enough to make you slow down, stand back and reflect. Many a time, as I fitted out my own boat *Sally*, a whiff of Davey's pipe saved me from some fatally irrevocable incision. Catching a nose-full of that aromatic mixture would freeze the saw in mid-stroke; hammer in mid-blow. It was as if Davey himself were standing beside you saying 'now if I were you...' He'd surely know why that plank fitted back to front. And if not, then it becomes not a simple mystery, or even rather mysterious but bloody mysterious, which is in a whole different category of mysteriousness altogether.

When an 'it' becomes a 'she'

Would you buy a 38-year-old wooden boat sight unseen? Exactly. That's what I told him. 'You must be mad. So the seller's a good friend of yours? So what. Get a survey. Go see it, at the very least,' I advised. 'Might save you a packet, not to mention your friendship.'

Did he heed my words? Did he hell. Off down south with a Land Rover and back he comes with this trailerful of 1965 Blackwater Sloop.

'I know why it's called a Blackwater Sloop now,' he says.

'Why?' I ask.

'Because it's full of black water and it's all slooping around inside.'

At least it proved he had a sense of humour, and I reckoned he'd need one. The bilge was six inches deep in oily water – an evil soup spiced with mouldy orange bunk cushions, spent flares, rope tails and greasy pigs of ballast. Black water soup (Ha! Ha!). The mast, once a lovely stick of varnished spruce, was blackened and peeling. The boom quite as bad. I didn't dare look into the sail bag just yet although my mate said that his mate had said 'they were in good nick. Nearly new, in fact'.

As for the engine, a little green petrol job cringing like a rusty frog under the companionway, maybe it had been a-whirring and a-spinning only three years ago, but to me it looked not so much like a Vire 12, more like a good mooring weight.

Next day the DIY accretions of 38 years took about 38 minutes to dismantle and hurl over the side: the vinyl insulation tiles glued to the deckhead, the ingenious fold-down chart table, flag locker, almanac holder, cup rack, swinging echo sounder bracket and the plywood galley which had been someone's pride and joy. Then we burnt it all.

Down below things were looking a lot better, despite the cracked timbers and the black mould. You could see the planking now (and some daylight through it) but at least it looked more like it had when Messrs Dan Webb & Feesey had built it in 1965, before a succession of loving, well-meaning owners had tried to improve it with plywood and foam-backed vinyl.

With the black water soup drained out via a two-inch hole bored in the port garboard, fresh air blowing through her, and the sun beating down she even smelled better. Why, for heaven's sake, we were even beginning to call 'it' a 'she'.

Among the debris were some surprising finds: strong wooden floors, not rusty steel, a Taylor's paraffin heater; two good anchors, plus lots of chain and plenty of fenders. And light boards, with her name *Bambino* carved nicely in them. Slowly, she was emerging from limbo. The little 18ft (5.5m) sloop breathed easier.

As for the trailer she came on, someone'd had already offered more than the price of the boat for that alone. So, I had to admit, my friend was already quids in. Double those cracked timbers, strip the varnish, replace the rubbing strip, recaulk a few seams. Nice winter project.

So, would you buy a boat unseen, even from a good friend for the price of the trailer? You wouldn't catch me taking a chance on a Blackwater Sloop I'd never set eyes on.

Except, for some reason, I did. That friend whose boat she was, was my friend. He'd bought *Bambino* and trailer for £500, then along comes another bambino, and suddenly she's too small for all the family. So he phones me; gives me the honest truth. Knows I'm in the business now. Building boats. 'The trailer's worth that alone, brand new, practically,' he says, correctly. 'And the sails have hardly been used.'

And when I opened the brown terylene bag, out they tumbled: mainsail, staysail and jib. Hardly been used.

The hissing of *Moonbeam*

They hiss, big boats do, as I discovered during the Fife Regatta on the Clyde while sitting down to leeward on the big cutter *Moonbeam*. A gust

came off the Argyllshire hills and she heeled to her gunwales, and a little beyond. It was that moment when the water cuts a line into the light-coloured teak, staining it black.

For a moment I was non-plussed; you don't associate sailing boats with hissing. Steam yachts, perhaps. Then I twigged. The hissing was of millions of tiny bubbles, smashed down by *Moonbeam*'s bow, escaping upwards at her quarters. They'd passed intimately along the full length of one of Mr Fife's shapeliest hulls; breath as it were held, and now being exhaled. It was the release of millions of little bubbles of breath. And as the power came on, so the hissing became louder. Like sailing in a sea of dark champagne.

Up forward on the bowsprit, where they were bending on the jib top, the sound would have been the more traditional roar generated by her bow wave and dolphin striker, the huge bone she was holding in her teeth. That's the sound we more commonly associate with ships. Where I was sitting she sounded like a huge sea snake, slipping through the dark waters in the Kyles of Bute, hissing like fury.

Make no mistake; these big pre-war cutters are awe-inspiring creatures. In a word, scary. *Moonbeam*'s mast goes up forever, then more, braced by a series of spreaders and struts and wires that make you understand why they called them Marconis. The men who sailed them in their heyday must have been strong and agile. Their skippers men of steel nerves.

Incredibly (should the Health and Safety people be told?) two wires appear to hold the key to whether this tracery of wire and wood comes tumbling down: the running backstays. As we came through the wind it was a matter of some urgency that the mainmast runner was made up fast and tight before *Moonbeam* bore away on the new tack. Oh, didn't I tell you? There was no winch. Just four men on the fall of a tackle.

So it was comforting to know they had a good man on the cleat: one of the best – the skipper of another Fife, no less. All that experience, just to take up a few turns on a cleat. But then again, anyone can haul down on a tackle – that just needs brute strength – but getting those turns on that cleat at the precise time is a job for a calm hand. At the crucial moment, he was the most important man on the boat.

Yup, these are crazy boats. Vast amounts of sail, a mast that depends on a cat's cradle of wires on a hull comprising thousands of pieces of timber held together by rivets, bolts, caulking and glue. A grand piano, a Stradivarius, a Sheraton chest of drawers hissing along at 9 knots. And hardly room to swing a cat down below. They are, in effect, the ultimate gentleman's conveyance: costly, impractical, dangerous, magnificent and gloriously useless. Thank heavens Mr Fife had the genius to design them.

Incidentally, taking a close interest in clinker boats, I derived as much pleasure out of analysing the line of the fine gig they keep on the deck of one of the big yachts as the vessel herself. After all that grandeur, studying something small and beautiful like a 14ft (4.3m) clinker dinghy comes as something of a relief.

And from the schooner *Adix* I can also pass on a good tip about clinker boat maintenance. To keep your dinghy plimmed up, hold a huge party every so often, and fill it up with iced water, beer cans and champagne bottles. Kind of wooden refrigerator. Cool, you might say...

Advice? No, therapy

Could he please talk to someone about his Laurent Giles? From his wallet he produced two grubby photos; before and after. 'Whatcha think?'

'So, a Giles dayboat, is it you've got? Pretty little thing,' I said, brightly, which cheered him up immediately. 'One of Giles's first glassfibre designs, if I'm not mistaken.' And that was about my sum total of knowledge. Like a man at a party, desperate to put a name to a familiar face, it was time to go fishing.

'About 1950, wasn't it? Built down south. Probably quite rare, but then again. A classic for sure,' I flailed as the London Boat Show hordes swirled around the stand, like a human tide around a rock (a wooden one) in a sea of, well, a huge sea of plastic.

'You think so?' he said, encouraged. 'I bought her a few years ago. Quite sad looking. But worth the trouble. The hull is sound. The rig's a problem. What do you think?'

'Have you tried Giles themselves? They're still in business,' I said, hoping he wouldn't ask me something technical about centre mainsheets or diamonds.

'They were helpful. Sent me a sailplan.' Ah, so no advice there. Must be the hull. Early case of osmosis? Flexing, was she? Crazed? Hogged? But no. He'd sorted all that. Perhaps he wanted to pick my brains about repainting.

'I expect she's looking a little tired after all these years,' I said, expecting questions about flow characteristics of two-pack polyurethane.

'Oh no, I've sprayed her and she looks like new. I'm now in the process of tracking down as many owners as I can. I've managed to find three from the early sixties, one of them still lives just outside Basingstoke...'

Of course. At which point, I confess, I let my attention wander, my eyes glazed. I allowed that beneficent, all-knowing, boat show smile to spread across my face and folded my arms, like a doctor. He didn't want advice about tuning the rig, antifouling, keelbolts or even some arcane nugget about the history of his boat. He wanted nothing more than to talk about her, with someone, someone willing to listen. He didn't want advice, he needed therapy.

Don't we all. It's what most old boat owners need. I've just bought a Land Rover, and the comfort value of knowing there's an owner's club and several magazines to help me through the dark days when the CV joint packs up or (God forbid) the gearbox fails is immense. It's the same with boats. In the dog days it's reassuring to know there's someone out there feeling your pain. Someone who shares the anguish of finding your bronze keelbolts have turned to cheese. And when she's more or less up to scratch, someone just to share her with.

'Course she's not your standard Vertue,' I hear myself saying. 'Fact is she's not strictly a Vertue at all. In those days she was just a little 5-tonner Giles knocked up for a client...' and so on and so on.

Manning stands at boat shows in a few years time we'll not need to listen at all; just take the name of the boat, nature of his problem, lead the poor fellow into a therapy booth and insert the right microchip. God help us if we make a mistake. Just wants to discuss his lovely Twister and we plug in the one about leaking garboards and the dangers of an overtight sterngland. Comes in smiling, leaves a gibbering wreck.

Classic bling

Gold plated. The winches on *Shamrock V* appeared to be coated in gold, or at least some electro-plated wonder metal that flashed like whore's gold in the sun. When Charles E Nicholson's 1930 America's Cup challenger overtook us the effect was dazzling, literally. It hurt the eyes as a succession of costly teak deck structures, cleats, winches, windlasses and stainless rigging swept past. It was like being overtaken by a truckload of reproduction furniture on a motorway.

Impressive though it was, I could not help comparing the sight with the Beken photos taken before the last war. And the comparison was unfavourable.

Gone was the clean, stripped spectacle of white, green or blue topsides and teak stained dark by the water foaming at the leeward rail, a single white lifebuoy perched on the counter. Gone the blinding white Egyptian cotton sails, stretched to perfection on wooden spars. Gone too the impression of fragile power, of a class that must always have seemed perilously close to the edge of technology.

Whatever happened to the great Js of old, that would cry off if the breeze was over 15 knots and whose masts would topple the moment it did? Of whom it was said that, if a candle flame held to the wind blew out, there was too much wind and if it stayed lit, too little? These overblown recreations, thundering down the white flecked Solent, with their carbon and Kevlar humming appeared to be in little danger of losing anything but a baseball cap or two from the afterguard. Something of the grandeur and danger had gone. It was as if someone had got their hands on one of Ettore Bugatti's spare blue racers, squeezed a Chevy V8 under the long bonnet, replaced the tyres with fat slicks and covered the fascia in walnut and Connolly leather.

Indeed of the 400 or so tonnes of metal and wood thundering past perhaps a tonne or two remained of the original structures: *Endeavour's* rudder post and some of *Shamrock's* planking. *Velsheda's* not even white now and her distinctive joggled plating has been smoothed away, all trace of imperfection airbrushed out like the publicity photos of a '30s screen goddess. For *Endeavour, Velsheda* and *Shamrock* read Monroe, Hayworth and Garbo, resurrected in some Frankenstein experiment using all the skills modern plastic surgery could devise.

This is churlish, you say. Nothing clever in the old J Class's fragility. They crossed the Atlantic under jury rig and did indeed lose masts and men in the kind of sailing breeze we saw at the 150th Jubilee. And thank goodness we have three of these most exotic of racing machines around in the 21st century. The cavernous bilges are overstuffed with generators, watermakers and air conditioning, but that's the price we pay to have them back.

Yet my eye goes back to those Beken photos. Black and white, yet never bettered. We know how Frank and Keith would wait in mid Solent in a stem dinghy for the Big Class to sweep by. Too far away and the shot would be missed; too close and row for your life. Maybe it's because the pictures they did squeeze off fill the frame, giving the impression of immense size, when in truth, even on the crowded Solent, three J Boats soon get lost in the mêlée.

And another more ominous thought. When last did we see such a display of ostentatious wealth and conspicuous consumption? And what followed the last flowering of these anachronistic machines? It was 1937 and the world had barely a year or so to enjoy itself before yachting became a memory, kept alive in the pages of much slimmed down journals by soldiers, sailors and airmen fighting far off battles. And afterwards *Endeavour*, *Lulworth* and *Velsheda* lay keelless in the marshes with no one giving tuppence for their former glory.

Yes, there was something eerily end-of-an-era about that display on the Solent. Something obscene. So much money flowing to such little real purpose. Those who benefited from the largesse this circus brought to town may disagree. It was not as if they had no clothes. Rather that, in their overstuffed, primped up finery these three empresses of the sea had too many clothes. And I was the small boy in the fable who watches the procession and dares speak what many others felt.

Eye of the beholder

There's a half model Peter Ward of Poole made of *Sally*, my little Vertue, in my study and on which I spend far too much time gazing. It is above my desk which gives me a diver's view of her lines, and it was while rubbing my temples the other day, searching for inspiration, that it struck me. Not in the sense of the model – which weighs about 5lb – falling off the wall, rather in how Jack Laurent Giles came to design her the way he did. It applies, I hasten to add, to all well-designed boats.

Above the waterline she has been drawn so as to appeal to us, the aesthete, the yachtsman; below she belongs simply to the dolphins, or more pertinently, to the water, which (let's face it) hasn't a clue about aesthetics; it just wants to flow round this annoying object, causing the least disturbance.

Quite obvious, really when you see a half model. There are two halves to a boat: the bit above the water and that which hides below. We see just the first bit; to the dolphins belongs the rest, and it is for the designer to ensure that both man and marine mammal are satisfied. Not easy.

Some designers can do it, others, often through no fault of eye or brain, cannot. If the brief has been for a 25-footer (7.6m) with a double cabin and standing headroom throughout, it's well nigh impossible, so they do their best. Moody 36? Hmm. Not bad.

To the designer in the 1930s, arguably the high point in cruising yacht design, working with a clean sheet, ('just design me a twenty-five-footer, Jack. Here's a fiver. Find a builder and I'll be back in the spring with the balance'), the challenge is delightfully simple. Above the waterline he must make her fulfil whatever notion of aesthetic beauty in yachts is current (and remember in 1893 they all said that *Britannia* looked ugly). In 1937, when *Sally* was built, that meant a sweet curve, a bold sheer and a little 'kick' in the sheerline aft, as if in apology or compensation for the abrupt advent of the transom (much cheaper to build) which cut off the natural progression of the lines. Below the waterline it's simple: she's a creature of the sea.

And yet, even in the best cases – think Robert Clark, Harrison Butler, Albert Strange – the hull above the waterline is only pleasing to the eye from certain viewpoints. But then it's only meant to be seen from certain viewpoints. The shape of a hull is so complex that it cannot possibly look good from every angle. That would be asking a great deal of a designer and of an object that must live successfully in two elements.

We only see a boat from sea level and occasionally a little higher; a quayside. But never as a whole, unless it's in the form of a half model in which case we can move from quayside, duck's-eye to fish-eye view, just by moving up and down in our chair.

So, looking at *Sally* again from a fish's eye view the sheer, so fair, bold and sweet, has become S-shaped. The boldness has flattened and begins to droop. Not unattractive, but still a little odd. But then who cares. Certainly not the fish. Meanwhile the canoe body from every angle looks gorgeous.

Which probably explains why *Sally* seems to attract so many dolphins. Obvious, really. Giles would say it was simply a question of matching aesthetics with hydrodynamics. Easier said than done.

Pyramids of necessity

'Call me Morgan.' OK, OK, it has not the ring of 'Call me Ishmael', the opening line spoken by Herman Melville's hero in *Moby Dick* but, at this time of the year when the days are short, the old urge to make some long sea passage, to cleanse the soul and refresh spirits dulled by long months spent ashore, is certainly common to us both. And to most of us who have a romantic notion of the seafaring life.

Melville's Ishmael ships aboard a whaler, the *Pequod* under Captain Ahab to seek the white whale – hardly a romantic notion. A year at sea to purge the senses of landlocked ennui, and a hard year, with no certainty of return. Being of somewhat weaker mettle I'd settle for a three-week passage to Antigua. No shorter, for it is only after a week or more at sea that one begins to feel its rhythm. Until then the habits and preoccupations of land intrude. Trivial things annoy. Not that trivial things don't annoy at sea, but they are different ones. Who the hell cares if your shirt's not ironed? A shipmate whistling *A Life on the Ocean Wave* all day long, now that's another matter.

On a long passage priorities change. We revert to a more primitive state. Not to say barbarous. It's a perfect example of the so-called pyramid of human comfort, the apex of which is the breath of life itself. Further down we find water, food, warmth and sleep until, near the base of the pyramid – now grown bloated with spurious luxury – we might find (depending on one's proclivities) such essentials as not missing the latest episode of *Friends*. A hot bath comes much further up the pyramid, though not, I confess, for me.

Whereas, on a boat, and I mean the smaller, probably wooden, ancient sort most of us go in for, the pyramid's base is small. The apex will be identical, but the base might simply comprise of a good book (with all the pages), a pair of dry socks and not being called by the watch for a sail change at midnight. It is an altogether simpler life in which the first priority is the boat. After all, breathing and sleeping will be short lived if you neglect to stem that leak.

And it is surely this reduction to basics that so appeals to us. On a short passage we are never far from shoreside luxuries. The longer we are at sea the more absurd these become, though we may dream of a hot bath and a bottle of Bollinger while someone rubs our back. That's part of the enjoyment; the dreaming. And we all dream of different things. Ironically, on land, I dream of being at sea.

Clearly, on that glorious morning as we approached the island of Barbados Neil, our shipmate on that long ago transatlantic passage, had been dreaming of a close shave and a clean body. No one noticed he'd disappeared below. When he reappeared in the cockpit the sight of his freshly scrubbed, wind-reddened face caused great amusement. Then, when he stood on the counter and we caught the first whiff of cologne, brought down on the Trade wind breeze our amusement turned to disgust. To this day I cannot recall anything worse than the smell of that aftershave. After three weeks at sea it was enough to send the rest of us retching over the side. Just goes to show that in the pyramid of necessity one man's luxury is another's total anathema.

2

'A Fragile and Unrewarding Occupation'

A drop of the red stuff

They'll be able to trace her builder from the DNA left in the form of a bloodstain just below the stemhead. It's hidden by the rubstrake but in years to come they'll scrape off that little patch of dried blood, put it under a microscope and match it to me. Every wooden boat built by hand and eye must have such traces of its builder hidden somewhere in the fabric, if only as sweat and, possibly, tears.

I seem to have shed a fair amount of blood on the loch boat I've been struggling to build up here at Ullapool Boatbuilders. And blood is devilishly difficult to expunge. Almost as bad as pencil marks. 'We were told at Lowestoft training college not to bleed on the boat or leave pencil marks,' was how Nat Wilson put it. So, the two substances so often left on a boat during its building – red corpuscles and pencil lead – just happen to be the trickiest things to get rid of. How typical of this perplexing trade.

From my DNA they will also know who was responsible for that breasthook joint that was less than hairline.

Frightening really: nothing you do is hidden for all time. When it comes to replacing a damaged plank the rivets will be ground off, the plank freed and laid bare for all to see. The bevel that wasn't quite accurate and the tiny split under the rove will be revealed for the first time since it was driven, possibly a little too energetically, home.

Which, to labour a point, is not the case in a glassfibre boat. Out of sight is out of mind. The wooden boatbuilder's sins will find him out. So, for the record, here is a short list of the defects that one day will come to light. I figure honesty is the best policy (and can only hope her new owner doesn't read this).

Aside from the bloodstain hidden under the rubstrake I can add the following:

1. In attempting to persuade the second plank to take the extreme curve of the transom, low down where it's at its most wineglassy, a teeny weeny split began to develop. It's no longer than a matchstick and packed with glue, so it won't go anywhere (and it's well supported by sternpost and knee) but it's there.

2. The third plank up is a little narrow forward, just where it begins to rise to the stem. 'Ah. That'll be a spiling error,' the old boatbuilder'll say in 20 years time when the plank is taken off for repair after she was run aground on a sharp rock. 'Easily done,' he'll say. Only a trained eye would spot that.

3. The line of rivets at the first mould wanders from true. Look closely and the spacing narrows from the required 3in to around 2in. Just three of them, and once again you'd never notice. Unless you built her.

4. Finally, that graving piece where the stem meets the keel looks great doesn't it? Proper job. Well, I have to confess that it's there only because the stem turned out to be half-an-inch shy of the bottom of the keel. So, in the best traditions of 'if you make a mistake, make it look like it's meant to be' we have that graving piece (which does in fact strengthen the joint). Again, it was not meant to be that way.

There may be a few more, but I'm not telling. When the DNA results come I'll be long gone. The transom might bear the legend 'Ullapool Boatbuilders, 2002'. I'd like to think that drop of blood is my personal builder's plaque.

Flat pack classics

'Hey buddy. That come as a flat pack?' The voice was transatlantic and coming from above and behind me.

'Suppose it might,' I said from beneath the boat, staring past the boots and up into the face of who I was only too aware could be a buyer.

'Only joking. Heap of work in that. Don't buy somth'n like that off the shelf,' he continued.

I agreed. A shit-load of work, to be accurate but not wanting to offend just nodded in a kind of weary, done it all, built-heaps-of-boats kinda way.

'You interested?'

He wasn't, but that didn't stop us chatting for a while as he peered inside. And it was only after he'd gone that I reckon he'd had an idea there. Flat-packed classics. 'Pak-a-Klassic. Let us do the hard work. All you need is riveting gear, screwdriver, mastic and paint. Be sure to read all the instructions before assembling. The manufacturer cannot be held responsible for missing knees, crooks or breasthooks.'

So, to see if it might work I deconstructed *Jan*, this Norwegian sjekte that's been growing slowly out back at Ullapool Boat Builders these past few months. Then put it all together again. Not the planks, or ribs, mind you. It would have been feasible if they'd been laid on without a bead of Arbocol between the lands, but you know how that stuff sticks …

Grind off the rivets; the ribs would have popped out no problem. And would probably keep enough shape in transit – 'we'll ship your boat any-place anywhere' – to pop back in again in Little Rock, Kansas or even New York where her predecessor, the first *Jan* was built, by one Karsten Ausland in the basement of his brownstone.

Interesting story this. At least I think so. Karsten (the Ausland refers to the town in Norway where he grew up) came to the US in the early 1930s and worked as a shipwright at Nevins yard. In his spare time he drew little boats that owed much to the craft he would have seen fishing in his native country. Yet his were no utilitarian craft. This was America, in 1934; the America of *Rainbow* and *Dorade*, Olin Stephens, Starling Burgess. The J Class. Lightweight aluminium masts. They were years of innovation. And Ausland was lucky enough to be working in America's top yard.

So *Jan*, I'd like to think, owes as much to Ausland's adopted country as the one he left. Viking in general form, it also has a Down East yachtiness. That bronze centreboard; that lofty sloop rig. Sjekte she may have started out as; little Yankee sloop she turned out. And from the papers sent to me by Anita Mason, whose father, the designer Al Mason, owned the boat – and who married Ausland's daughter – it seemed she gave good account of herself on the waters off Marblehead. Even beat old L Francis Herreshoff's new skiff coupla times. Flat pack? Flat pack? No way. Hey, we're dealing with history here.

Only smells remain

The first layer stripped gave off the synthetic smell of the 1990s – a blend of epoxy, trowelled hopefully into widening fissures, and hot International polyurethane varnish. The old GP14 would have been well down on her luck by this time.

Deeper still I came to the '80s when an authentic restoration would still have been possible; the rot in its infancy. But we were all too busy making money and spending it ostentatiously. The layers of cheap, brittle paint flaked off too easily, exposing a harder crust. The 1960s, surprisingly, were far from flaky.

Refurbishing an old wooden dinghy reveals much about its past; how she was built and how she was cared for. The filled screw holes speak of tweaks and gadgets fitted and discarded in doomed efforts to live with the club leaders.

By the time she comes to me she's just a cruising dinghy, neglected but not forgotten. Certainly still loved, for the memories. One day we'll get her back on the water. For the kids. For old time's sake. All she needs is a little bit of time, and care. If only we had the time.

Paint and varnish: the smells are redolent of each phase in her life, until way back under the hastily applied enamel, the quick repair with body filler and glass mat, you arrive at the birth. It is like uncovering a vase buried under millennia of mud and rock.

Thus stripped lay the GP14. There, finally, I came upon bedrock – the hard layer of Copal varnish, warmed and thinned, applied by an old hand with a round bristle brush reused so many times, cherished and put to bed

after work like a faithful hound. I could only admire the skill of the men who had put her together, and the quality of the materials they used. The plywood was flawless after 50 years; the pine stringers intact. Even the glue was holding. There was efficiency and huge skill here in the building of this GP14, one of hundreds.

Some time ago, at a conference in Liverpool, I asked, 'What makes an authentic restoration?' The panel boxed the compass trying to pin down the answer. The extent of the old structure remaining, perhaps? Maybe it was enough simply to enclose the original space, replacing plank and frame piece by piece?

The debate ranged far and wide, until a quiet voice from the end of the table spoke up. I think it was Greg Powlesland.

'Gentlemen. In my opinion what makes an authentic restoration is whether the old smells remain.'

There was a moment's silence. Here was the man who had restored the Victorian cutter *Marigold*, and his own *Collinette*, from truck to keel using traditional materials and methods. The bunks were stuffed with horsehair, the decks caulked with marine glue, the sails cut from cotton. It was not, then, the rake of the mast, or the number of original planks but the smell that made these boats authentic.

Ah, the smell... I am back now in my grandfather's garden where an old green clinker dinghy lies upturned, baking under the sun, and I'm playing with the hosepipe as my father begins the spring repainting.

For ultimately it is the smells that stay, rekindled by a hot air gun played on old paint; the odours of the past, of sun-filled days under Terylene sails, sun on hot varnished thwarts, the ripple of water when this little dinghy was new and her crew thought her the best thing, just the most exciting thing.

Fragile and unrewarding

Find me an amateur boatbuilder who doesn't aspire to stand alongside time-served professionals in a working yard; handle the big machines; turn a pile of timber into a hull; steam and rove up straight-grained oak; craft gunwales, thwarts, knees and finally launch the fruit of months of intense labour (and hours of sleepless nights). In short, to live the nostalgia, the romance of wooden boats ...

Whoa. Romance? Nostalgia? After 12 months working alongside the partners at a busy traditional yard on the north-west coast of Scotland, I have to confess that this ancient and increasingly anachronistic occupation is – as the designer and author John Leather (who died in 2006) suggested in a letter I am sure he won't mind my quoting – a 'fragile and unrewarding thing to do'. 'Nostalgia' or 'romance' did not appear in John's *Pocket Oxford*.

Now I take his 'fragile' in the sense that profit margins are as slender as a Dragon's bow and for financial rewards you would indeed be advised to look elsewhere for a career. Oscar Wilde famously said that to make money and gain status in this world simply apply yourself, study hard and become a lawyer. While most people can be a lawyer, not everyone is cut out to be a boatbuilder. A year down the line I have built two boats, and the biggest compliment paid to me (and ever likely to be paid) was 'not bad for a journalist'.

That does not, alas, make me a boatbuilder; it takes more than the skills to shape a plank, spile accurately, cut a bevel or steam timbers to call oneself a boatbuilder. Apart from the ability to weld, sister a frame in the depths of a rotting fishing boat, cut a thread in a piece of aluminium bronze or make a set of moulds from a photocopied lines plan you need to get on with all your colleagues, avoid wastage and, above all (although time spent thinking about a problem is indeed time well spent) cultivate speed.

Alas, on the first two counts. As to the third, I must have spent four months out of 12 thinking; which is far too long. Most people with some manual dexterity can build a 15ft (4.6m) clinker dinghy to a reasonable standard in five months and sell it for £4,000. Taking materials into account, say £1,500, that leaves £2,500, or £500 a month. That's £6,000 a year. Hmm. Sharing the running costs of the yard – perhaps £150 a week – and you'd be losing £1,800 a year. No, the secret is speed. Turn out a boat in five weeks and it begins to make sense. Albeit fragile sense.

I have learnt a huge amount in my time at the yard, and yet at the back of my mind lurked the knowledge that my livelihood did not depend on building boats. To be brutal: if I had been doing it for a living I'd have gone bust in the first six months. Which makes the bravery of the handful of traditional yards that still eke out a fragile living in the country all the more admirable.

Until people are once again prepared to pay honest money for an honest wooden boat, and crucially pay up on time, keeping the flame alive will depend on amateurs. They can take the luxury of spending three days polishing rivet heads. Trying new ways to do things done for centuries one way. Above all they can afford to be romantic. For the yards it will always be a question of watching the pennies and the clock.

And yet I have a sneaking suspicion that no boatbuilder ever quite believed he was 'just doing a job', toiling from daybreak to sunrise in a draughty shed turning out objects of desire for rich yachtsmen. Fragile and unrewarding it may have seemed, yet the best of them must have clung to some sense that what they were doing was more important than the work of a lawyer, bringing home more in a week than they could in a month.

What about that old fellow who stopped by the yard last month, the one who built lifeboats for the *Queen Mary*. Was it just a job? In which case, after building hundreds of boats, why had he taken such a keen interest in mine? Surely the R- and the N-words. Sadly, in a business where the difference between profit and loss can be the price of a box of roves, romance or nostalgia, however essential ingredients, are not enough.

My first boat

I'll be building one next week, a sternpost that is; for a 15ft (4.6m) loch fishing boat, my first. She'll have a beam of 5ft 6in (1.7m), stable mid section, curved forefoot easing into a straightish, gently raked stem and the transom – a thing of great beauty – is taken off an old pulling boat, beyond redemption but an inspiration still. No one has the heart to burn her, so she sits on her port bilge runner, sprung stem and all, outside in the cold holding water after all those years. You can just hear the chorus: 'They don't build 'em like that...' But they do.

It began as a story for the *Independent*. The idea was to spend a few weeks working alongside a traditional boatbuilder in the Highlands. Ah, the romance of it all. The smell of Stockholm tar, the sweet reek of Cuprinol, wood shavings curling like pasta twirls knee deep on the floor, a collie curled up by the wood burning stove, a great ship growing day by day in the centre of the shed, rafters groaning with spars, the swish of adze, tap tap of the riveting hammer, gentle banter of craftsmen going about their work (OK, I may have laid it on a bit thick). It worked.

'Sounds great. Our readers will love that,' enthused my editor. 'Everyone dreams of doing something mad.' Then, 1,000 words later I'd slide back to The Smoke.

Except it hasn't worked out quite like that. Two months later the article's written and I'm still here, with a bench full of new tools and a dusty overall to my name. What have I got to show for it? A pair of spoon oars and a rapidly strengthening right arm. What began as a story has become a lifestyle. In six months I might even begin to make a living out of it. I'd better do. With the constant temptations of the Axminster and Screwfix catalogues to hand and a company call Highland Industrial Supplies in Inverness not 40 minutes away (just imagine a warehouse the size of B&Q full of tools that takes credit cards) I'll need to make some money soon to pay for that jack plane, angle grinder, cordless drill, set of Stanley chisels, bevel, block plane, etc that arrived by courier the other day, followed a week later by a credit card statement for £385.94 (inc VAT).

At the moment it's a case of trying to pretend I know what I'm doing when, in truth, everything's new. 'Ever used one of these before?' asks Mark, Gill or Tim handing me something with knobs and a spindle that spins at 32,000rpm. 'Oh, way back. Just remind me. They've changed so much since then.'

Frankly it's embarrassing how little I know about things I've been writing about for years. Remember that series on carvel boat building? Cynics take heart: your worst fears about journalists are correct; we do know nothing, and what we don't know we make up. Whereas these guys, when it comes to stem joints, plank butts, aprons and sternposts, know a great deal. Plus quite a bit about transcribing a Bach cantata for guitar, nursing and the geology of Peru.

Which reminded me of Colin Mudie's observation, that medieval boat builders were the rocket scientists of their day, so far removed from the rest of the populace as to be in a class of their own. They still are. This lot, up at Ullapool Boatbuilders seem to confirm that. I won't say which of them went to Cambridge and studied geology, who the nurse or who the trained concert soloist (they are smart but so modest) but believe me there is not much they don't know about.

Then there's myself. Profession: hack. Apprenticed at 40-something to a firm of traditional boat builders. Learning to build boats. At the moment, eight weeks into my new lifestyle, it is very definitely all rocket science to me. Must dash, I've a nose cone, sorry, transom to fair up.

Downshifting

Undertook a little marketing exercise on behalf of Viking Boats International (Ullapool) plc a few weeks ago. Nothing fancy, simply a press release about the boats, nice photo and a note to editors explaining briefly how I came to be building wooden boats in Scotland after a life of city drudgery.

Rather than highlighting the importance of keeping tradition alive, larch and oak, ancient skills, blah blah, I'd aimed it at those with big houses with lakes: 'Little Viking Boats for Lakeside Homes' (for the Scots, lakeside became lochside). So, having identified my new, lucrative market, I awaited the deluge of press coverage and was looking forward to telling customers that 'due to demand I couldn't promise delivery until the spring, of next year that is'.

Alas. The phone remained silent. The *Daily Telegraph* and 29 other national publications, ranging from *Country Living* to the *Inverness Courier* had clearly not been impressed. Zilch. *Nada* or, as the Dyson carpet sweeper ads go, 'Not a sausage'. In one word: vacuum. Maybe the

idea of building wooden boats was so outlandish as to be ludicrous? Perhaps I'd got the emphasis wrong.

Then came the email. From a nice woman at *The Times*. Intrigued. We'll take 1,000 words. Even pay you to write them. It sounded good. Paid to tell the country's top people how brilliant my boats are?

Well no. Turns out features woman interested not so much in the labour of my calloused hands, the extreme craftsmanship of my lapstrake or the subtle curves of my steaming, but about me. Foolishly, buried somewhere in my press release I'd used the word 'downshifting', a word sure to perk up any jaded newspaper features editor looking for a Saturday fix. I'd downshifted to Ullpool from the big city, and was now building wooden boats. She did not want a boatbuilding story but a downshifting story or 'piece' as they say in Fleet Street.

My 'piece' was to be about why and how we made the momentous decision to leave London and downshift to a godforsaken wilderness somewhere on the fringes of civilisation. Of life among humble crofting folk, where milk came in pails and all subsist on rough oat cakes and the occasional haunch of venison (poached from under the noses of fierce Highland ghillies from the local estate). The bucolic idyll, in other words, of Fleet Street fantasy.

So I obliged. After all, there was £250 in it for me and, if I could work it into the piece subtly enough, a free tweak for my fledgling business. Thus I waxed on about hills, lochs and long days out fishing; of my shed by the water where stout wooden boats emerged from rude planks of timber. I skirted the unpalatable: that Ullapool has two supermarkets, a Boots, several pubs, two bookshops, an arts centre, fitness centre, swimming pool and golf course. That it has a parking warden and broadband. Instead I painted a scene of rural tranquillity, where life was lived the old way. Where water came off the hillside, and the postie always stopped for a chat.

The last is true. She will also as likely as not know the contents of your post, and when the other day I received my first (unsolicited) copy of *Saga* magazine, it was round my friends before I knew it.

And the response from my piece? A flood of orders? A commission to build a 30ft (9m) cruising boat? Zilch. Not a sausage. Just a call from a literary agent. 'Would I consider writing a book about...' (be still my beating heart, wooden boatbuilding perhaps?). Nah. He wanted me to write a book about, you guessed, 'downshifting'. Bit depressing really.

Boats, buttocks and bums

It's awfully difficult to avoid double entendres when you're talking boats' bottoms. Maybe it's just my puerile sense of humour; the more grown-up among you will just have to grin and bare(!) it. Besides, this is more about up-ending than bottoms. Whichever, the bottom being up-ended was that of the little Norwegian sjekte, *Jan*, I've been building these past five months and the embarrassment all mine.

Finally, three weeks ago, we turned her over – we being myself and the three partners of the firm of boatbuilders up in the village. Now there's a knack in shifting boats as anyone knows who remembers the days when yards would use greased baulks of timbers – hollows and rounds – to rearrange the yachts in their care prior to launching. So best, I thought, to bring in the experts.

The manoeuvre took some planning; the execution was swift. For five months I'd only been able to admire her interior, as first the ribs, then the gunwales, thwarts and floorboards went in. For the first time I would have an uninterrupted sight of her underside, in its full glory. For the first time we would *all* have a glimpse of her bottom, and it was a moment that every boatbuilder will recognise; it's the moment when all is revealed. For five months her extremities had been modestly hidden from view. No longer.

I'd like to think it was akin to gazing at Jennifer Lopez' bum, among the world's most perfect if you believe the tabloids, for the first time. 'Among the most perfect' being the key, for as she flipped, four pairs of eyes took in at an expert glance every nuance of her shape. And not only her shape. Traces of cellulite; bumps and hollows (planer marks). Reckon you get the gist...

The collective scrutiny lasted no longer than a few seconds; ten at the most. And in those seconds, 50 years of boatbuilding experience managed to take in every blemish and imperfection. I'm sure I saw Mark cast a critical eye over the overall shape; Gill was more interested in the finish. Jo was keen to see how much mastic had been used in the lands, and I? Well I was relieved just to have her flat on her back at last.

Nothing much, of course, was said. Nothing ever is. A few grunts of appreciation, for she is, despite my efforts, a creature of extreme beauty and her bottom a sight to behold. Now the moment had passed. The embarrassment was over. We could draw a veil over *Jan's* bum, in other words.

Then it was eyes up and small talk. Ten seconds had been all that they needed to assess my efforts. Further scrutiny, in boatbuilding etiquette, would have been impolite, even offensive. Worse than taking a magnifying glass to someone's rabbet or running a hand ostentatiously over some prize varnishwork onto which a gust of wind has blown half the loose sawdust in the shop.

So what is it about boats' bottoms, then? Other people's boats. How often have you sidled over to something on the hard and had a quick deek (as the Scots say) at her garboards? Poked about at her hood ends?

Wiggled her wobbly pintles? Yes, there's something undignified, vulnerable about a boat exposed for all to see.

Certainly, gentleman that I am, if there'd been a sheet handy as we turned *Jan* over, I'd have whipped it over her keel for modesty's sake. Then, when everyone had gone, I'd have had a quiet peek. Ripped off her skirt, run my hand over her planks and, yes, stroked her bottom for the first time.

Oh for Pete's sake. Get a grip.

Burning boats

You can make many claims for traditional boatbuilding methods, but ecologically sound it is not. To howls of protest let me explain.

Who was responsible for the deforestation of England's great oak forests? The shipbuilders. And of India's teak forests? The same culprits. What happened to perhaps the best of all boatbuilding timbers, the pitch pine? Stripped out of the forests of North America. And New Zealand's Kauri? And Baltic spar timber?

Today we make do with larch that our forebears wouldn't use to feed the wood burner, and it's getting scarcer by the year. Acres of quality teak are taken illegally to clad the decks of super yachts and every five years or so the owner demands it's replaced – suntan lotion is so disfiguring.

No, steel, if its manufacture did not entail so much expenditure of energy (aluminium even more so) is a better material, ecologically sounder. And so is glassfibre, after all (despite all the warnings of shortages) there seems to be plenty of oil left. Besides, what would you rather see: a stand of 200-year-old teak felled or a few barrels of 20,000-year-old oil pumped up from the ground?

Wooden boatbuilders can make many claims; wooden boats are more satisfying to build, better in a seaway, more tactile, sweeter lined, etc. What they shouldn't try and justify is the ecological credentials of their methods and materials. Put it another way, if all boats were still built in wood, we'd have a world shortage that would make the deforestation of the past centuries look like careful management.

It is simply – and I would argue only – because wooden boats are so scarce that we can indeed claim that we are doing no deep harm to the environment. We don't build enough of them, thank goodness.

For, be under no delusions, a wooden boat is hugely wasteful. Half the volume of that larch and oak seasoning in the corner of the yard will be transformed into sawdust, shavings and offcuts for the wood burner. Simply planing that $5/8$in plank down to $1/2$in loses 25 per cent; spiling out the curve accounts for at least another 25 per cent. And the wastage goes on. Keeping the yard warm by burning costly timber may save on electricity, but it's not exactly efficient. Better to build an energy-efficient yard, double-glazed and well insulated, than heat a draughty shed with precious larch. But we do. It's 'traditional'.

So how many cubic feet of prime boatbuilding timber has gone into raising the temperature of our traditional yards a few degrees over the centuries? How many tons of timber have been turned to ash? How many tons of combustion gases belched up the chimney?

For all we might castigate the builders of glassfibre boats, their energy efficiency, insulation, dust extraction and air-conditioning would shame all but the best equipped traditional counterpart. Their workers are better protected and their wastage is minimal. Can you imagine a corner of any modern production yard given over to a pot-belly stove, fuelled by offcuts of glassfibre, around which chilled workers huddle over mugs of tea?

The yards that survive today seem to have inherited many of the bad habits of their predecessors, and added a few of their own. Instead of a mist of oak dust we have a fog of mastic and epoxy, synthetic paints and isocyanate glues. Boatbuilders of the last century knew no better. Life expectancy was not good. What would an environmental officer have made of such a miasma of dust and white lead? No ear defenders, goggles and just a handkerchief over the mouth.

Only the efficiency of today's breathing masks, goggles and ear defenders lies between today's wooden boatbuilders and those of the 19th century. And, as always, more than half of the raw material goes up in smoke.

Building by numbers

Who'd be daft enough to build a faering in any way other than the traditional Norwegian way, ie without moulds, by eye, using sticks braced against the roof joists to keep the strakes down and an axe to cut the scarphs? Me; but then I'm not Olaf, and this is not my 300th faering. If it were then I'd heft a razor-sharp hand axe to cut the scarphs and bevels, and set up the stem and sternpost to ancient beams, and employ sticks on which my father, grandfather and great-grandfather had marked the measurements of every faering, and variation of faering they'd built since 1860.

This, you will gather, is my first faering. The brief called for 'a faering-type shape' but it's turning into a true faering, thanks to the genius of designer Iain Oughtred. I can't now get away with anything less than a precise replica, which is why a sheaf of plans arrived by post from the Isle of Skye last month. They leave little room for interpretation. Every plank land is marked, every dimension noted. This is not the way they built faerings, and it is not the way I am accustomed to building boats. But it does work – if you stick to the plans. Stray and woe betide.

Nevertheless, it is a crazy way to build a simple old boat. Like using offsets to make a dugout canoe. See, I can't make it up as I go along. The garboard, shaped like a double scimitar, was made from a plywood template. To make plywood, throwaway templates smacks of wastefulness. And yet I do not have those deceptively slow old Norwegian boat builders' time-learnt hands, or strake patterns in my head, or a shed where the precise height from every beam to every plank land is known. If I am to make a decent fist of this faering, I cannot do without Iain's careful plans. And this I find disturbing. Will someone please tell me why?

How much better to build this most simple of boats the old way. You want to know how? I'll tell you, from a 13-minute film shot in the 1960s, in black and white, inside a wooden shed near Bergen.

First hoik up some lumps of oak, seasoning in brine under the floorboards (your shed is built over the fjord side). From templates carve out the stem, in two pieces. Scarph (using just an axe) and rivet. Do same for sternpost. Shape and set up on rough wooden blocks, and posts braced to floor joists.

Shape keel with axe to take garboard and scarph to stem and sternposts. Line all up using string and a pair of dividers held at eye level (to set the angle of the garboards? Who knows).

Get out twisted fore and aft garboard sections from solid using a pit saw. Nail to stem and sternpost, and rabbet, holding plank edges down using sticks to ceiling and from floor. Scarph garboard pieces together. Cut bevel using axe. Fit and scarph next strake. Joggle in frames, fit sheer strakes, rangs, thwarts, etc. Cover with pine tar and launch. How is the shape of each strake determined? By eye? Ancient templates? Search me. Nowhere did I catch a glimpse of a plan.

I am having immense fun building by numbers. Must save an awful lot of time; time being the most obvious difference between the faering I saw being built on the scratchy old film and mine. Mine will take just three months. What's that Olaf? Did I hear you say three days…?

Plywood phooey

So farewell, in the style of *Private Eye's* EJ Thribb, Ted's Boat. Or, to be accurate, *Florence Oliver*, the names of Ted's grandchildren who, come spring, will be frolicking among her timbers, lifejacketed and wellie-booted, playing Vikings.

This, the second 18ft (5.5m) sjekte I've laid my hand to in 12 months, has occupied every waking, and most sleeping, hours since her keel was

laid back in June. Now, around 80 working days later, she's ready to head south. Next month she should be at the London Boat Show, baring her all to public scrutiny.

Clinker boatbuilding is not for the faint hearted, and I can well understand why so few are built these days. Out went solid timber, in came plywood and epoxy. And, at the risk of offending some high exponents on the technique, it's a great shame. I've read the manual for epoxy ply and, to be frank, very few of the techniques have any relevance to clinker, there are as many pitfalls in building boats this way as there are traditionally, they deteriorate just as quickly, are hard to repair invisibly and can't take neglect.

Don't get me wrong; a well-built epoxy ply boat is a pleasure to lay eyes upon. Take a look at designer Iain Oughtred's own *Jeannie II* if you've any doubts, for she is a thing of extreme refinement, expertly executed. And she sails like a witch. But, at the risk of offending the very highest exponent of the technique, what's the point? The Vikings built light and strong, in the pursuit of rape and pillage, and Uffa Fox took the art of dinghy building to further heights in pursuit of pot-hunting the world's championships. Just because clinker is tricky doesn't mean it shouldn't be attempted by skilled amateurs, from whose ranks I feel justified in saying that I have, after three years, finally graduated.

So, I don't know it all; heaven forbid I should ever claim that, but I know enough to say with some authority (and plenty of passion) that, given basic skills and enough time, a clinker boat, built in the old way, is not difficult. The finished article is no more than a sum of relatively straightforward stages: the keel, the stem and stern, the rabbet, the garboards, the thicknessing of the planks, the bevelling, the geralds, the riveting, the steaming of the timbers, the gunwales, the stringers, the thwarts and the painting.

And there's not a globule of epoxy in sight; no sealing of the end grain, no filleting, no mess, no mixing, and no scarphing of arbitrarily short 8ft (2.4m) lengths of standard, and expensive, plywood.

Has the result of my 80 days been worthwhile? Pore over the line of planking, riveting and the accuracy of the joints. Quiz me over my method of spiling off (I reckon it's a step forward) and why the centreboard box was built that way, and my views on varnish. For, despite appearance, *Florence Oliver* is not totally traditional. Having read a little, listened a lot and lain for hours closed-eyed in the bath thinking, I have gone my own small way in some small matters, moving the plot on, I'd like to think, incrementally. However, she'd still be instantly recognisable to a Viking boatbuilder.

With the departure of Ted's Boat comes the arrival of an 18ft (5.5m) Blackwater Sloop. Now that the plywood of 30 years' ill-informed DIY has been jettisoned her structure lies bare. And if there are any readers planning a similar restoration, or even a little 'improvement', may I make a plea? Firstly, unless it's 15-year guaranteed Bruynzeel, bin it. Second, avoid epoxy unless part of a well researched re-decking operation; third, use only bronze screws – even today's brass is suspect – no A2 stainless below the waterline, and certainly nothing with a Pozidrive head designed for chipboard. Don't screw anything to the basic structure of the boat unless you must. And please, no polystyrene tiles, glued laminate flooring, plastic cable clips, vinyl cushions, brassed light fittings screwed to the coachroof or strip lights. Instead, find something authentic at the boat jumble; salvage some old mahogany; recycle some pitch pine; use some of the teak from the old village hall floor. When in years to come someone comes to restore her they'll salute your stewardship.

Of boats, backs and ballerinas

Darcey Bussell; now there's a name to conjure with. So swift, so effortless, so lithe and elegant. Ah Ms Bussell. Beautiful ballerina. What would I do without you?

One of the lesser known benefits of becoming a boatbuilder is the variety of people you meet during the course of your work, folk you'd never normally encounter. In my case, among them, a child psychiatrist (useful, I learnt a lot about myself), an aircraft builder (both sides of the boat should match), a poet (hark, I hear the sound of chisels), three writers (two a penny), an adventurer (penniless unfortunately), several members of the landed gentry (also, sadly, in reduced circumstances) and a legendary ballet dancer.

Of these the latter is not only by far the most comely (as they used to say) but also quite possibly the most beneficial, long term. Now it would be wonderful if the former principal ballerina of the Royal Ballet were to commission a boat from me, but I doubt she will. Her contribution to my well-being is not financial but purely physical. Darcey Bussell, bless her sequinned tutu, has become a daily and indispensable part of my life. We spend our mornings together, on the floor; and before you jump to any conclusion I am talking Pilates. Darcey and me, or to be honest, her book *Pilates For Life* has become an essential part of my daily warm up.

Until the stabbing pain woke me at three in the morning, just after Christmas, I was invincible. Strong in arm and back I'd leap out of bed, dress, wash, shave (once in a while), gulp down a pot of tea, wolf a couple of slices of toast, vault into the Land Rover, race to the shed and within seconds I'd be into whatever I'd left off the day before. No stretching, no exercise and certainly no girly warming up. From bed to cold boat shed in 15 minutes flat. Oh the eagerness of the amateur.

At first I put it down to simple muscle strain. I'd hobble downstairs and by the time I'd had my second cuppa things had eased off. It was a warning sign, which I ignored. Until the pain struck.

Much is written about the nuts and bolts of building boats, scarphs and joints, but little about the dangers (apart from the warning notes printed

on paint and glue tins). You'll be aware of the toxic dust, and the fumes from isocyanates. And possibly the dangers of iroko. Falling off ladders is an occupational hazard, as too are amputating fingers in band saws and routing bleeding grooves in various parts of your body. Those who fancy themselves with the adze should look to their shins, and table saws can also bite back. But for sheer pain I can't imagine anything worse than a night spent writhing around with a bedfellow called sciatica. I'd rather, as they say, have needles shoved in my eyes. Serves me right for taking up boatbuilding at my age and serves as a warning for anyone out there who reckons they, too, are invincible.

Things are easing now, thanks to Dr Weekes (my GP), a chiropractor in Inverness and Darcey; her glute-building exercises are inspirational, and the way she demonstrates the cat position, ahem, inspiring. My gentle warm up with Darcey every morning, preferably before the double-dose caffeine shot and the first Golden Virginia roll-up, seems to be doing the trick.

Thus it struck me: Darcey and the old codger in the brown overalls working away steadily in the back of his shed, have much in common. They both pace themselves. They take frequent breaks for tea (or Evian water), they never seem hurried. And their work is so swift, so effortless, so lithe and elegant. Reckon she'd make a better boatbuilder than I'd a ballet dancer.

‼@‼#

In space no one can hear you scream. On a farm only the chickens hear you swear. And the pigs. Which is just as well, for down at the farm by the lochside where stands the old milking parlour I proudly call my shed, a good deal of swearing goes on that probably wouldn't if there were other than livestock around.

Now working alone has its attractions, viz: you can take your tea break whenever you like (or not); you can borrow your own tools (and blunt them); play Radio 3 at high volume; hurl broken light bulbs at the wall; do slightly dodgy things with epoxy and sawdust when you leave small gaps, and above all swear as loudly and profanely as you want whenever you like.

All these factors make for a happy working relationship and, as a rule, I rub along pretty well with myself, time flies, and the job gets done, I'd like to think, rather more quickly than in the company of others.

Whether it's healthy to spend so much time in one's own company is for others to judge. And certainly it has its downsides. For instance there's no one to second-guess a problem, pass things up or shake a head in sympathy when the plank splits or you tip the box of roves into the varnish pot. No one also to make the tea, no one's bread and cheese to nick, and no one to borrow a fiver off. Working alone you have to figure things out for yourself; and if you left the drill on the bench you'll just have to get out from under the bilges and go fetch it.

On balance, having tried both, it's better working alone, unless you find yourself part of one of those once-in-a-lifetime teams. Alone you can console yourself that, like a struggling artist in a garret, it's traditional. Not however overly romantic. When starving poets die, clutching slim volumes of Keats, fellow artists grab their brushes and immortalise the moment of expiration. Cussed old blokes in brown dungarees and pokey old sheds coughing their last out in a cloud of wood dust and Woodbines have never featured prominently in any art gallery I've patronised.

We are told that in Shetland there are hundreds of boatbuilders who would all be making a living if the price of timber wasn't so stupidly high due to carriage costs from the mainland. Further south I know at least five who toil in isolation. One's building a 34ft (10.3m) carvel cruising yacht in a huge shed that once rang to the sound of many shipwrights' hammers. Sometimes it's colder inside than out in winter, and stifling in summer. Farther away from that slick new boatbuilding training facility in Falmouth with its dust extractors and heating ducts it would be hard to imagine. Seems as though boatbuilding and draughty sheds go together.

Draughts I can live with, and making my own tea, but this swearing's got to stop. So I've invested in a new stereo system and have taken to playing Mozart continuously throughout the day. It's virtually impossible to swear when Lucia Popp's singing the Queen of the Night aria from *Magic Flute*. Music does indeed have the power to soothe the savage boatbuilder.

Failing that I may have to buy a parrot. Just for the company. We could share our sandwiches; go flying; compare notes on the pros and cons of scarph joints and resorcinol glues or discuss John Donne and the metaphysical poets (for this would be an educated bird). But he'd have to watch his language. The chickens have grown used to the air turning blue, but it's not fair on the piglets.

The beauty of asymmetry

A fast forward video of Morgan, manic boat builder, over the past few weeks would reveal a blur ascending and descending a precarious ladder propped up beside a Folkboat outside a cattle shed on a farm by a sea loch in the Highlands. The sky would rapidly cloud over, rain would obliterate the scene, followed by bright sun, followed by more rain (in fact mostly rain). The grass would fade. Pigs would rootle about, and grow fatter by the minute. Chickens would appear as a squawking swirl and sheep in the field beyond as a diaphanous Airtex blanket on a coverlet of green. Cars would pull up and shoot off, tractors unload bales of straw as the life of the farm unfolded rapidly round about.

Nothing much, however, of the boat itself would change – bulkheads would fly up the ladder and come back down again a few dozen times. Engine beds likewise. You might even catch sight of a Yanmar diesel whizz aloft and be lowered onto the engine beds by fork lift. A few frames later, accompanied by another frantic blur (that's me unscrewing the bolts) the engine will disappear again upwards (along with the beds). If a microphone were to accompany the video it would reveal frequent and unrepeatable profanities (as if uttered by a demented chipmunk, and thankfully indecipherable, for remember we are watching in fast forward).

In fact that's how I have come to see myself – a demented rodent. It beats me how anyone ever finishes the interior of a boat, but they do say that the hull is barely a third of the work in a restoration project. I can verify that. Interiors require a whole different set of skills – those of a shop fitter; albeit one who can fit straight stuff to curved bits, first time, maybe just one dry run, and to curvy bits that in an old boat are apt to vary between port and starboard.

Now here's a thing. I'd made a template of the main cockpit bulkhead, starboard side, from cardboard. The companionway was central, so the template would do fine for the port side. Wrong. The companionway was at least an inch, more like two inches offset to starboard, for which there can be no excuse. It makes no difference ultimately; the eye does not detect the difference, but it made me doubly careful. And sure enough the more I measured the more discrepancies I discovered. The forward bulkheads likewise are not symmetrical, the fore side of the coachroof is squint, the mast is offset and, most worryingly, the chainplates on one side are two inches further forward than on the other. And this is a boat built by a highly reputable yard.

But then again, why should I expect any better? When Elkins built my boat in 1937 they must have put the apprentice to work on the port side and the old man on the starboard (or vice versa) for she, too, is not symmetrical, as I discovered when trying many years ago to scribe the waterlines side for side. Again it makes no matter, and I cannot say that *Sally* goes better on one tack than the other. She steers herself equally well. Nor can I see any difference, but knowing it makes her the more special, more human in a funny kind of way.

It's a bit like Kate Moss's face. What makes it so intriguing is not the perfection but the imperfection. Very few supermodels have perfect features; they have quirks, whether it be a squint nose, prominent mole or some other tiny imperfection. Thus I concluded that humans prefer flawed

to perfect beauty. It's what defines beauty in humans. And when our super-models behave badly, we just love them the more. Can this be a metaphor for old boats? Asymmetrical and quirky, we love them for their foibles rather than their perfection? It's certainly worth thinking on.

Boating building is cool, or rather, cold

Gloucester Old Spots and Percy the wild boar are my companions down at the farm by the shores of Loch Broom where I build wooden boats. The field above my shed is awash with sheep who converge pathetically on my Land Rover every morning (you can't expect a sheep to know the difference between the shepherd's 2.5 litre Td5 diesel and my 200 series Tdi). All is idyllic. Pete comes with his pail to feed Percy mid-morning and check on the piglets, Tam who's building an organic vegetable garden, stops to pass the time of day and there's always the chickens to chase from the shed where they take refuge overnight from the farm dogs – two collies who behave well alone and like wolves when allowed to roam together.

This, then, is the quintessential, traditional boatbuilding scene. Rural tranquillity, a brisk tapping of roving hammers (split by the occasional scream of the thicknesser), the grunt of pigs, crowing of cockerels, clatter of sleet on corrugated iron roofs. This is why I left the city. This is what every commuter stuck between Blackfriars and King's Cross dreams of on a Friday night in June when his boat's already lifting to the tide off Pin Mill.

And yet it makes no sense. The traditional boatbuilding industry in this country is hanging on by a waisted keelbolt. You'll find pockets of expertise all round our coasts – a yard here and there which can still do competent wooden boat repairs – but nothing on the scale of what you would find on the east coast of the America.

Now I have visited New England three times, and not to look at wooden boats. It was in the 1980s when Australia was edging closer to winning the America's Cup. On the strength of the advertisements in *WoodenBoat* magazine the sheds – they call them shops – by the waterside, are alive and throbbing. To slip a canvas apron over your lumberjack shirt, stick a pencil behind your ear (and a few more in your special pencil pocket), strap a tool belt round your waist, hitch up your denims and make with the Lie Nielsen bronze smoothing plane is, well, cool. In Old England it's crazy.

Naval architect John Perryman told me something odd at the London Boat Show apropos wooden boats: 'It is a strange fact that a furniture maker need only mark up his chair 300 per cent and people think it's more valuable. A wooden boatbuilder has never been able to ask a reasonable price for what he makes.'

Did you know that Camper & Nicholsons never made any money from building boats? So what hope have we?

I write this having just quoted for another 18ft (5.5m) clinker double ender. That's 60 days work, plus materials, costs, rent, overheads, sails, spars. What does £8,500 sound like? The phone goes quiet for a moment. He's thinking 'Strewth, that's a lot for a little wooden boat? I could buy a brand new Fiat Punto for less than that. Or two Plastub simulated clinker rowing boats, or a Drastic Plugger.' And he'd be right. Off the shelf, delivered tomorrow, comes in blue or green. Why in heaven should a production line glassfibre boat for £8,500 sound reasonable and a handmade larch on oak clinker boat of the same length that took three months to build 'a bit steep'? Beats me.

I have a theory – several in fact:

Number one. The myth of maintenance. Wooden boatbuilders (and I don't mean plywood and epoxy) have been too slow in espousing new technology. We have microporous water-based varnishes that last for decades; we have flexible mastics that ensure a clinker boat will not leak, ever. Yet we persist in slapping 50/50 varnish on bare wood, and wonder why it's peeling by next spring.

Number two. People have bought the myth of glassfibre. It's too late to convert all but a very tiny minority. Glassfibre is now the traditional boatbuilding material (just as steel makes cars). Forget it.

And thirdly, they think we just do it for fun. They think we enjoy spending our days in and around draughty old milking parlours on the shores of Highland lochs, with piglets and cockerels for company, listening to Mozart on the radio, passing the time of day with farmers and market gardeners, laying coats of enamel on smooth topsides and shaping larch into perfect curves...

'A tenner and she's yours ....'

A friend of mine, artist, in an abstract kind of way, of international renown, sells his paintings on the never never. Works like this. Go in to his studio, clap eyes on a few paintings, one in particular perhaps. 'Strewth, but that's fine,' you think (that's 'God's truth' by the way; I've been asked to explain it several times). 'But £1,500? I could buy a new Wykeham Martin for the old girl for that, and a pair of bronze sheet winches from Classic Marine.'

Then Paddy my painter friend hoves into view. 'So, d'you like it? Then take it away wid yer.' (I've laid that on a little thick, he's a perfectly civilised Irishman, with just a trace of the old country). 'What can yer give me now?' he'll say. 'Make it a tenner and she's yours. Just pay me what you can when you can.'

I've had several paintings off him on that basis. Fact is he's sold most of them like that, and last time I saw him he told me that he'd never, in more than 40 years, had anyone

renege on a payment. Regular as clockwork, the little sums come through the post, in fivers here and tenners there. I tell a lie: there was a snag one time. A fellow bought a painting cash down, and never came back to collect it.

It sounds like an idea I should take up as I can't bear to hear any more people saying 'she's a lovely boat but a bit out of my price bracket'. Gor blimey guv'nor ('God blind me, governor') how come you can slap down a deposit for the same amount on a poxy BMW and plead poverty when it comes to a piece of artistry that took months, not three German robots three hours, to make?

I've touched on this subject before, and will do again, as it lies at the heart of the wooden boatbuilding revival. Commission a chair from Viscount 'I'm the Queen's bleeding cousin' Linley and you're looking at a few grand, and he rarely even lays his hand on a spokeshave these days (so my royal mole tells me). Might as well commission my supremely talented friend Dan, who works at Tim Stead's studio in the Borders to make you something really, really fine (I know that for a fact because he also has a classy old wooden boat which he's restoring).

Oh the injustice of it all. Was it ever thus? The fruits of man's hand, the sweat of his brow and peanuts to show for it? Why is it that a photographer can flex his little finger and pick up a grand a day, and I'm on £100 (at best)? Arrange some bricks in a nice pattern and Tate Modern will bung you £50,000 (from the tax payer).

Now this faering I've just delivered is a work of art as well as a practical vehicle for getting her owner and family around the east coast creeks. That should make her worth double that vase with no bottom (a useless vessel).

But life is not fair and boatbuilding has never paid the bills. So I am curious to try a new approach: taking a leaf out of my late boatbuilder friend Robb White's book (he never set a price or delivery date) and my painter friend Paddy's (who is happy to wait ten years to get full payment), I propose to operate thus. From now on I will not give a price, or delivery date, and will encourage my owners to send me whatever they can afford for however long they feel inclined to send it. Like that restaurant where you pay what you reckon the food's worth. I expect to be opening small brown envelopes containing fivers and tenners in a steady trickle from now on. And I'll also know (when the trickle stops) exactly what any of my boat's are really worth. Come to think of it, that restaurant went bust in very short order...

3

The Fury of Inanimate Objects

£23,000 for a rowing boat?

Heard the one about the fellow who dragged his boat up the shingle when the Met Office forecast a hurricane; staked her down safe, well above the high water mark… and a tree fell on her? Not so funny, in reality; you indicate, check your mirrors, pull out and nature's juggernaut side-swipes you, or in this case a lone pine takes out your starboard side, four planks down, leaving a roughly tree-shaped hole.

But every cloud, or force 12, has a silver lining, for it has been left to me to fix the hole, and I like nothing better than to make good the ravages of time in good old boats, and this is a good 'un.

She was built about ten years ago by Topher Dawson, formerly of Scoraig, now head of maths at Ullapool School. A man of many parts, Mr Dawson – Edinburgh, Cambridge, Scoraig and living proof that my theory which holds that Oxbridge graduates are only good for pushing pens in Whitehall, keeping the flag flying in far-flung parts of what used to be the British Empire or self-destructing spectacularly on drugs, alcohol (or both) but writing amusing, well-crafted books about the experience, is total rubbish.

Topher is a born non-conformist. How many people do you know who've built half a loch Fyne skiff – long story – or a clinker-ply car based on a Citroen 2CV, but with three wheels? He also designs and builds windmill blades. And it was a delight to find that the same precision was employed in the construction of the tree-felled boat that awaits collection in my shed after 56 hours of remedial surgery.

I just knew that when it came to scarphing in the new sections I'd find them so sweetly curved. The batten merely caressed the marks on the spile board, describing a gentle arc which looked right from the start. A good honest boat of the kind that were turned out by the thousands in the good old days before we got all precious about wooden boats.

Now I don't want to cast aspersions – well I do really. Let's just say that we could do with a few more examples of Topher-type boats. That's not to say that finely crafted examples of the shipwright's art, gleaming under 19 coats of burnished Epifanes, with rivets that line up like a troop of guardsmen aren't impressive – they are. But just look at the price tag? Take that exquisite pair on show at the London Boat Show in 2007. Flawless, they were. Immaculate isn't the word (though I don't know what is). I couldn't find a single trace of a chisel stroke that had gone awry, just the evidence of one falsely drilled hole, artfully plugged, and almost undetectable to the naked eye. But £23,000 for a rowing boat? Does not that give an ever so slightly skewed impression of wooden boats?

No, by all means let's have the apprentice piece that took half a year to build; the master shipwright's best effort and the exhibition piece, but let

us also encourage some more, shall we say, down to earth examples of wooden boat building, more affordable, less intimidating, but no less skillfully crafted. Just not so, hmm, pernickety's the word. Precious would be good too, given the cost.

In the days when wooden boats were two a penny builders were skilled at producing good boats fast. And the more they built, the faster they became and the better they became. Practice made perfect.

Not all were good boats, of course, and some were atrocious, as much due to flaws in engineering and design as in building. The late John Leather – never a man to wear rose-tinted glasses – delighted in picking holes in West Country-built craft, for example. 'Weak under the mast step,' he'd say. No, he preferred properly designed, which usually meant Essex-built, craft. But he also delighted in (and designed a few) good workaday boats, built by honest hands for an honest trade. Nothing fancy, just tarred on the inside, painted white on the outside, strong and sweet lined. Like the one in my shed.

Familiarity leads to lost fingers

It's a dangerous business safety. Every time I use the planer it's a case of: 'OK Morgan. What's it to be? Asphyxiated by oak dust, blinded by a wood chip or deafened. You choose.' I go through phases. One day I might put on the whole shebang: ear defenders, mask and goggles. Other days I think: 'what the hell'. Some days I won't find my mask for hours, and when I do it's caked in dust. I shake it, put it over my mouth and inhale a day's worth of dust in one gulp.

Then there's the question: in what order do you put on your safety gear? Strap on goggles first and the ear defenders fit no problem. But the mask? No. So it's off with the lot of it – like trying to put your shoes on before your socks. So it's mask, goggles, then ear defenders.

Oh that it were that simple. The mask, no matter how careful I am, is always full of dust or moisture (or both). The goggles are never crystal clear, and over glasses it's like looking through grubby double-glazing.

Which means I can't see much. Which means I often can't find my ear defenders. Especially when it's hot and the fug from my mask steams up my goggles. Before I've put on the ear defenders I'm staggering around with my hands out, tripping over things.

Put the ear defenders on and I'm deaf. Thus deaf, half blind and breathing heavily I grope towards one of the most lethal, yet innocuous-looking pieces of boat shop equipment: the bandsaw. I press the green button, and a faint whirring noise become apparent. I push the workpiece against the blade and nothing happens. The whirring noise was the fridge in the deer larder kicking in next door. I have not plugged the bandsaw in.

And so it goes on. And so I have to choose. Do I want to hear the bandsaw, and not see it? Or vice versa. Do I value my lungs over my eyes, or my ears over my sight? It seems that I cannot have all three. Mostly, as I already wear glasses, I leave off my goggles — unless I'm grinding steel. When I'm grinding wood then it's mask, no goggles and ear defenders.

As for the planer, which emits a banshee shriek that is probably responsible for keeping my shed mice-free, my first recourse is to the ear defenders. I figure the chances of a wood chip getting past my glasses is slim, and how much dust can a planer make?

The other day, when a weak sun slanted through the skylights, I discovered that a planer does indeed make a huge amount of fine dust. The shed was a miasma of suspended dust particles. It was as if I were the meat in a huge pot of dust soup.

Today I resolve to wear at least two out of my three defences: I will wear a mask mostly, and ear defenders whenever it gets noisy. That way at least I'll not be coughing my way to an early grave holding a brass trumpet to my ear. My eyes? They'll have to take their chances, unless I'm attacking metal with a grinder. The thought of a red hot sliver of steel in my cornea doesn't appeal.

As for the bandsaw, I reckon that not wearing ear defenders is probably the safest bet. The times I've left it running, and not realised I nearly couldn't count on the fingers of my hands (I nearly lost them, that's why). I am reconciled to losing one sooner or later, as I have developed a morbid fascination with that singing blade. Like a man who must stand on the very edge of a precipice, I dice with disaster every time I fire up the bandsaw. The other day I found myself fishing small slivers of wood from beside the blade – without stopping the damn thing. They say that over familiarity with machinery is the cause of the majority of accidents. Well me and my bandsaw are, you know, just like that. She calls me Posh and I call her Becks (it's an Elektra Beckum). And you can't get much more familiar than that.

The fury of inanimate objects

If ever I write a book about sailing, which is highly unlikely, *The Fury of Inanimate Objects* will be the title. Why? Because on a boat you are surrounded by inanimate objects, all apparently out to get you.

And it's worst at the beginning of the season. It's as if the boat is trying to remind you how long you've neglected her. Thus, with a bang on the shin, crack on the head – whatever's her favourite trick – she'll reassert herself. Let you know who's boss. Remind you to look after her. That flogging sheet; the bowline that just won't untie; the damned spanner that slips on the godforsaken cylinder head nut. Some days the boat bites you as if to say 'Watch it. Don't you ever take me for granted'. Inanimate they may be. That does not mean they and the paraphernalia needed to make them work don't have lives of their own.

In the scheme of things the wind should not be categorised as an inanimate object. It moves. Poets, and the ancients give the impression that winds have life; Zephyrus, etc. (One day I will use this space simply to recite Kingsley's *Ode to the Northeast Wind,* the one that would drive brave English sailors down Channel to fight great sea battles). But the poet is wrong. At sea the wind tops the list of things that can infuriate, indeed it is the most infuriating. Therefore, by my definition, inanimate.

What must it be like to live on one of those perpetually windy islands in the far north or deep south, Shetland, Kerguelens or Falklands, where the constant whining can drive one insane? There's a continental wind that causes madness. Anyone killing during a Levanter can claim mitigation. I've read that the screaming of a hurricane can induce a feeling of abject terror and anger at its senseless fury. Oh Lord my ship is so small...

I remember nearing Dartmouth, coincidentally on a black night in the teeth of a northerly, funnelling fiercely out of the estuary. The feeble outboard was trying its best. (As a classic example of inanimate object I suppose we should have been grateful that it deigned to start at all). We made it only by dint of tacking, under power for there was no chance of *Galway Blazer's* Chinese rig working us to windward, eventually creeping into the entrance and shelter. Not before I had cried out in the darkness and screaming of the wind: 'For god's sake, give us a break!'

Can one ever become inured to the sound and the fury of a gale? At sea the wind conspires with all loose things to create a kind of mayhem. Like the ringleader of an infernal orchestra the wind goads its minions into insubordination. Below the tins bang and rattle, the pots leap about and locker doors, supposedly securely fastened, burst loose. Want another example? Drag the jib, flogging and protesting down the forestay and the halyard will entangle itself on the upper crosstree. Stumble aft to the mast

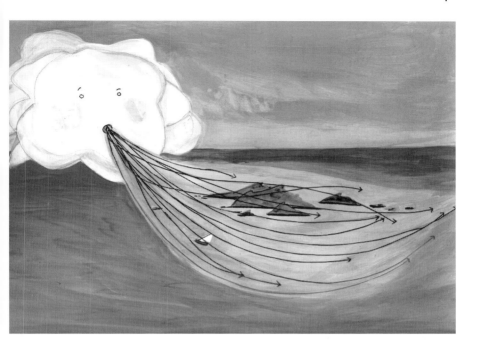

and attempt to capture the bitter end and, like as not the jib, seizing its chance, will fly up the stay at the wind's behest. Stagger forward and the anchor windlass will catch you on the shin. And of such small annoyances tragedies are made.

It's easy to say 'rise above it'. The best seamen manage it. It demands a kind of patient acceptance, allied to a determination to prevail. Ellen MacArthur has it, so did Knox-Johnston, Moitessier and the rest. I'm not sure that I can, however much I try.

Tom's rules of thumb

Sometimes I feel like shouting 'is there anyone out there?' Then along comes a letter from Tom Whitfield which makes it all worthwhile.

Tom's been a wooden boatbuilder all his life, serving his time in Devon before emigrating to Australia, where he ran his own yard for many years. His rules of thumb are based on the kind of experience I cannot hope to achieve in the one score and (maybe) ten allotted to me. So, here's a few master tips from a man who very clearly knows.

Whitfield's Rules of Thumb
Clinker planking for a 12ft (3.6m) dinghy should be about $3/8$in thick, with a $3/4$in lap, ie 2:1.

Plank widths should be no more than 5in plus the $3/4$in lap, the narrower the better.

Nail spacing should be six times the plank thickness, as should scarphs, both 6:1.

Outer end of scarphs should have a butt about $1/16$in on $3/8$in planking, 6:1.

Ribs should be placed at every second or third nail spacing.

Plank joints should be at least three plank or three frame spaces apart.

Ply scarphs to be slash cut and glued, 8:1

Mast or spar scarphs to be about 10:1 or, better still, 12:1

Rowing seat height should be no less than 10in above the floor.

Seat risers should be 7in from sheer plus 1in for the thwart.

Rowlocks should be centred 12 $1/2$in aft of the back edge of the thwart.

Oars need to be 1 $1/2$ or 2 times the beam of the boat.

Working oars: the blade should be about $1/3$ the oar's length.

Racing oars: the blade should be about $1/4$ to $1/6$ the oar's length.

A boat's length to beam ratio should be about 3:1 or 4:1, although I have built good boats with a beam half the length, ie 2:1. Cornish gigs are about 5.33:1. Racing eights are 12:1.

And, finally, rivets should have a rove 1 $1/4$ times the head size of the nail. Allow a bit less than the width of the square of the nail projecting through the rove to allow riveting.

So here are mine:

Morgan's Rules of Thumb
A thumb's width between anything that should be close fitting is far too big to disguise (even with thickened epoxy). Don't even try.

In any case, a thumb's width is a useless measurement in a boat, being not quite an inch and certainly not 'yeah big' (whatever that is).

The crucial tool is always an arm's length plus a thumb's width away, ie just out of reach.

The instant you worry about hitting your thumbnail with a hammer, you'll do it. Try to forget them.

Finally: keep thumbs away from bandsaw blades, to which they are fatally attracted. Try to remember them.

As far as general rules go:
Dropped chisels (like buttered toast) will always fall edge down.

That lost pencil is not behind your ear (nor are your spectacles on your nose) and furthermore the tape measure is not where you left it.

Time spent looking for a misplaced tool is time well spent; you'll not find the tool you lost today, but the one you lost yesterday. But don't despair: the one you lost today you'll find tomorrow, and so on.

You can never have enough small drill bits and yet, drill bits, in the smaller sizes, are always just too big or fractionally too small.

The bandsaw or grinder you bought from Axminster or Screwfix will be on special offer next week, and cheaper still at Machine Mart.

The ratio of glue that finds its way onto hands, overalls, hair and spectacles, to glue effectively used for gluing is about 2:1.

Finally: measure twice and cut once. Discard, measure again and cut (but it still won't fit).

Professionally speaking ....

It began with what sounded suspiciously like a compliment which, coming from Joe, is rare. Like all professionals he's sparing with praise. Just as journalists never say: 'saw your piece, really liked it', boatbuilders, in my albeit limited experience, seldom say anything more than: 'reckon that'll do the job', certainly not 'really loved your half-lipped scarphed dovetails'. Maybe in America, but not here. We reserve our enthusiasm for mistakes, as in 'nasty looking split in that plank, see. 'Course, the whole lot'll have to come off.'

So, when Joe sauntered over and peered at the engine box I was laboriously constructing I wasn't expecting lavish admiration for the brilliance of my joinery. 'Hmm,' says Joe. 'Solid job, that.' (See what I mean?) And then, sure enough, looking at my hands, again at the box, the killer line: 'sponsored by Balcotan, is it?'

Now Balcotan is a glue, as you will know, invented by a shoemaker and now used extensively by boatbuilders for all but the really crucial stuff. For it is good, with just two nasty habits. Get some where you don't want it and it boils up like Vesuvius and is the very devil to scrape off. Get some on your hands and they turn black. Which is as much a giveaway as the invisible ink they put on dodgy pound notes to see who's been handling them. Basically it sorts the honest from the criminal. And in the same way Balcotan sorts the professional from the amateur. In other words you seldom see a professional boatbuilder with black hands. Nor do you see a professional painter with paint-stained overalls (or hands for that matter).

So, sayeth the Great Boatbuilder (*The Book of Bob*, chapter 7, line 3) 'by the colour of their hands shall they be known and by the state of their overalls shall ye judge them'. Amateurs are just as capable of building fine boats, achieving fine finishes, but the difference is how much glue and paint they spread around in the process. And how many tools they mislay.

And there are other differences. Watch a professional. Doesn't seem to be

hurrying. Always time for a chat, cup of tea. Nothing seems to be happening then: bosh, job's done. No fuss, no flurry and no Balcotan on his hands.

Take tools (no don't; professionals never lend, and seldom borrow, tools). Mine are never where I want them. Climb aboard boat to measure up for engine box, discover pencil is on bench. Descend ladder; retrieve pencil; break pencil and discover clasp knife is also on bench. Descend ladder, etc. In the course of a simple job I can put in several miles of needless walking. A time-frame sequence would have me zigzagging the yard like a demented collie. Train the same camera on Mark or Joe or Gill, however, and you'd see no movement at all (expect when tea's up). But look how that plank in the foreground miraculously gets fitted, roved up and painted.

Let's have a detailed look again at my engine box. Cut mitred oak frame on chop saw, so far so good. Drill corners for screws; fine. Reach for the Balcotan; stop. Put on disposable gloves; good, you remembered. Apply glue to joints. Smear glue with gloved finger. Snag rubber on screw. Glue runs inside rubber glove. You see? The rot's set in already. And the trouble with Balcotan is that if you try to wipe it off early with white spirit it distributes itself evenly over both hands, turning them a uniform dark grey rather than black.

Finally, having glued up the frame I remove gloves and stand back to admire work, before putting away hand drill and glue bottle. Too late. Drill grip is covered in Balcotan. So is the Balcotan bottle. Go home in despair.

Next morning I arrive at work to discover that, apart from having Balcotaned my drill onto the bench, I have also glued the trigger solid and, for good measure, the drill bit into the chuck. Now tell me, and be honest. Which of you professionals have ever done that?

Cast off your shackles

'Chuck out your chintz.' It was IKEA I recall which coined the phrase; a phrase that was to launch a thousand skips. And, d'you know, the Swedes feel the same way about fussy soft furnishings as I do about shackles and bottlescrews, those expensive connectors we habitually use to join bits of our rigging together. What's wrong with string, I say? Lanyards, lashings, strops, webbing, etc? Why this mania for the shiny stuff? Why this magpie craving for baubles – expensive ones at that?

An example. A while back I came upon this nice new clinker yawl. There were these two bowsprit stays, stainless, fair enough, with Talurit eyes and thimbles. But in order to attach them to the bronze bowsprit end

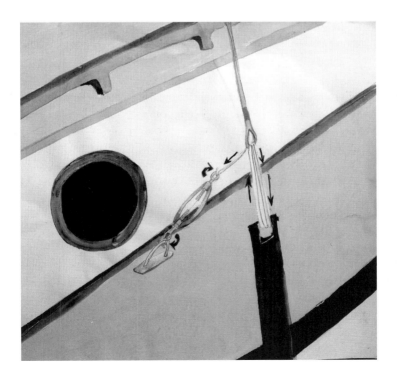

fitting (what's the name of that, someone?) and bowsprit plates, the owner had stumped up for six stainless shackles, and two bottlescrews, when a piece of string – we call every rope on our boat string, but I'm sure there's a word for the stuff, lanyard will do – would have sufficed to attach whisker stays to eyes. Oh, and there were more shackles and bottlescrews for the forestay and the bobstay. Tensioning a lanyard may have been a lengthier business, but all in all the simplicity wins hands down. And what of the cost of four turnbuckles and ten shackles? An extreme case, admittedly.

Sally has far fewer shackles than when I first found her. The first year I showered her with shiny bits, which in subsequent years were stripped off. She now has a shackle bin, or rather a string of redundant shackles a foot long. Anyone for a brace of $^3/_8$ in, captive pin-twisted bows?

One place where string is not only cheaper, simpler but safer is for joining guardwires to pulpits, and pushpits, a term Bernard Hayman, my old editor on *Yachting World*, abhorred. ('No such thing; they're stern pulpits, Adrian.') Join guard wires with shackles and bottlescrews and there's no way you can cut them quickly to heave up a man overboard.

Furthermore, if you can get away with it, and your boat's of modest size, then consider binning those bottlescrews and use string to attach shrouds to shroud plates. Then you can discard not only the connecting shackles, but those extravagant Swiss bolt croppers you bought at the boat show; replace them with a serrated kitchen knife – the equivalent to the sailorman's axe used to chop away the shrouds on the old square riggers when pressed down by the weight of canvas in a Southern Ocean squall.

This came to mind recently when we sailed back from the Faroes aboard *Eda Frandsen*, a gaff-rigged former Danish fishing boat that charters the Western Isles and beyond. She has lanyards and huge lignum vitae dead eyes which, in extremis, could be hacked away if the rig failed. Big string, basically.

Where's this all leading? Search me. Maybe it's a plea for simplicity, to throw off the complex and embrace the straightforward; the wetted finger versus the masthead wind vane, the sextant versus the satellite. An old argument, but worth repeating at Boat Show time. Pass those cut-price electronic merchants by, and head for the rope stands. Feast your eyes on multiplait and pre-stretched nylon (Cor...!). Fondle a skein of small stuff (Blimey...!), or sniff that tarred marlin (Mmmm...!) Reflect on the endless possibilities inherent in that bin-end of 5mm Hempalon.

As for me, I will be heading for the Garmin stand. Is *Sally* the only yacht with a GPS held together with black electrical tape and waxed whipping twine? You can take this string-driven thing only so far.

4 Here be Dragons

Racing? Heaven forfend

Competitive? Who isn't? Although by nature I am more the weasely type who prefers, given the chance, to sneak up on the blind side to cries of 'Blimey, where the hell did he come from?'

Years ago I entered my old National 12 *Fesquie* for the Burton Cup, the big class trophy. We turned up in Falmouth with a boat we reckoned was the business; freshly varnished, new sails... until we saw the competition. There was Jo Richards (who now designs America's Cup yachts) fettling his Twelve in the dinghy park – 240 wet and dry, rig tensioner, telltales, NACA section rudder blade in Neoprene protective cover... We'd only just rigged a Cunningham, never mind understood what it did. We didn't stand a chance.

First race we placed last; ditto the second. On the third day we were again trailing the fleet and decided to chuck it in. We'd not had a hot shower all week. The water had always been stone cold by the time we arrived back.

Then, 100 yards or so from the beach, *miraculoso*. Out at sea I noticed the fleet lay idle. Inshore the wind was ripping up little white horses. To hell with hot showers. We soon had the old girl on the plane and storming towards the windward mark.

The orange buoy and glory beckoned. I could see it clearly.

From the *Daily Telegraph*: By our special correspondent

MORGAN MAKES HIS MOVE

A brilliant tactical move by Adrian Morgan saw *Fesquie* jump from dead last to first to win the National 12s' most prestigious trophy in Falmouth yesterday. While the favourite, Jo Richards, struggled to make the finish, Morgan and his crew swept to...

... when the wind died. For us, at least. Our private breeze had now been appropriated by the rest of the fleet. I can hear the roar of their bow waves even now as they rolled over us like a herd of wildebeest. We were again dead last and the showers were again stone cold.

I've since raced many times: Channel Races in which you never saw a thing, other than the flash of some godforsaken buoy in Lyme Bay; a day and a night spent sitting on the rail of a Half Tonner, dodging spray and wishing it were over. And the slowest Fastnet on record (I read four books). And Cowes Week, at the wheel of a Swan 41, late for the start and they called for the big tri-radial – as a 40-knot squall struck. It came down in shreds. 'You've just cost me four thousand quid,' says Bruce, the owner. 'Give me the helm...'

The closest I've come to racing in recent years is the annual Scottish Traditional Boat Festival at Portsoy, a jolly affair set amidst the granite backdrop of an 18th-century fishing port. Of course it's not serious racing. Lawks a'mercy, no. This is fun. And yet, I maintain, that only by taking racing seriously is it ever fun. There is no such thing as a 'fun' race (unless it's popping balloons on buoys or picking up toy ducks or sailing blind-folded, or…). Put two boats alongside each other and sooner or later helmsmen will be tweaking jib sheets and tightening luffs.

So when people say 'don't take it so seriously' I wince. How can you take a race anything other than seriously? As to those who moan 'but our boat doesn't go to windward' I reply: 'then get one that does'. We may sail old boats, or replicas of old boats but that's no excuse for slack luffs and saggy gaffs. Our forebears raced for their lives every day in boats like ours to scratch a living. Look at the perfection of that big Zulu's dipping lug. It's no fun to arrive back with your catch spoilt and the fish train departed. Makes missing a hot shower look very tame.

Sheep-shape

I did the postie in our little village in the Highlands a disservice in one of my columns, apparently. Gets off her bike and tells me in no uncertain terms (she's Australian by the way) that she also has an honours degree in – now I wrote this down verbatim somewhere – 'late 19th century Catholic social literature studies', I think it says, but then my hand writing's indeci-pherable, even to me.

Which brings me in a (very) roundabout way to our new address. The view from the windows is essentially the same – wide, deep valley, hills rising beyond, big sky above, wooded hillside behind. Except that we've swapped ripples for sheep. In fact we've swapped riplets, wavelets, small waves, crashing breakers and blown spume for sheep. The valley we now overlook is not flooded as before, but a pastoral scene of such idyllic beauty that it brings to mind Bach's *Sheep May Safely Graze* (unless Bran the darling German shorthaired pointer suddenly takes an interest).

Living by the sea, overlooking water, is many people's dream. Me? I was brought up staring at the stuff in all its grey beastliness. The sea never stands still, like sheep. Constantly on the move, reinventing itself. Restless, unsettling. When sheep move it's never in an unsettling way, like waves. In the old house, one look at the loch and all thoughts of going sailing would flee from my mind. 'What, go out in that?'

When we lived in London, and my view was of a Brixton side street, the weekends could not come quick enough. And after a drive of two or three hours it didn't matter what the sea looked like. I couldn't wait to get the sails bent, drop the mooring and head seawards.

Those who live by the sea – and it's only a theory of mine – probably do less sailing than those who live in the cities. It's like climbing; most climbers seem to live in Manchester, in fourth-floor flats (presumably so they can always shin up the drainpipe if the urge grows too strong).

Now that I have sheep not waves outside my window I am looking forward to getting afloat a lot more often. Given the choice between woolly creatures gently munching down in the valley and white horses cavorting down the loch in wild herds, snorting and steaming I'd take the former every time. Don't get me wrong. On water is where I feel most at ease. It's simply that I don't care to see it outside my window every day.

And talking of sheep, how many farmers are sailors? The remarkable Willie Ker who used to sail his Contessa 32 *Assent* to the Arctic most summers comes to mind. I once interviewed Willie and found him smart in reasonably fashionable, albeit slightly small, Henri Lloyd oilskins. It was only near the end of our time together that he told me they were borrowed for the occasion. Normally, he said, he sailed in farm wear – you know, the classic green body warmer, green wellies, green PVC jacket and trouser look that would get you thrown out of the Royal Yacht Squadron quicker than you could say blackball. 'Nothing like wool next to your skin,' he told me. See? Sheep again – the common theme running through this month's ramble.

Which brings me finally to my friend Neil up at Rhidorroch. Neil loves his sheep, and his Highland cattle, rolling acres, etc, etc, no question, but also keeps a Laurent Giles 43-footer. A beautiful boat; strong, seaworthy and built in teak by Moody's at the peak of their wooden boat powers in the 1960s. Rhidorroch is also up a long glen, miles from the sea. After a winter of feeding, worming, gathering, dipping, shearing and other sheepy chores I know for a fact that he can't wait to get afloat. Must be the view.

Catch 'em young

We launched young Ally off in the 7ft (2.1m) dinghy and watched him splash around, feeling oars for the first time. He'd seen his father do it, so it couldn't be *that* hard. More often than not the blades would hit the water like a fish slice and Ally would rock backwards, grinning. Sometimes one oar would make contact, the other wouldn't and the little plywood dinghy would spin round. 'He can't come to much harm. The worst that can happen is he'll get a soaking,' said his father. Ally was, of course, wearing a lifejacket and had more or less got the hang of it by the time he'd drifted perhaps 50 yards off from the mothership (should that be father-ship?).

Then, emboldened by his success, he flailed up to the boat, obliquely, like a wayward water beetle, shipping his oar expertly as the dinghy came alongside. He'd picked that up from his father too, as he couldn't possibly have seen the bit in the Hiscocks' *Wanderer III* film when Susan demonstrates the correct technique while Eric supplies a running commentary in those wonderful clipped 1950s tones.

In a little over ten minutes Ally was proficient enough to carry a passenger; his little sister Freya was hoisted aboard and off they paddled, oars windmilling, Ally grinning, Freya getting accustomed to sitting regally in the sternsheets, trailing a languid hand in the limpid waters.

'That's how it must start,' I thought. 'The bloke gets the first crack with the oars, the girl is thrown in as ballast and that's it. The pattern's set for life.' In 15 years time she'll be ensconced coyly in the sternsheets of a skiff, all straw hat, floaty dress and parasol, with some young chap at the oars wracking his brains how he's going to pop the question.

And how quick they seem to learn, given the chance. There was minimal parental interference that warm June morning. Just the confidence to let them have a go, make a few mistakes and get the hang of it in their own time. No shouting, no instructions, no tether line. After all what harm could they come to in a flat calm little bay with three adults at hand?

Soon Ally and his sister were heading for the shore, some 100 yards away as confident as you please. 'The worst that can happen is they'll get a soaking,' said their father once again, slightly less confidently, as Freya scrambled onto the seaweedy rocks and the dinghy's bow shot up into the air. It was too far away and hidden by an outcrop to see whether they used a bowline, a round turn and two half hitches or just a scrabble knot to make the painter fast, or what they made it fast to. Probably a strand of seaweed. They were off and up into the birch trees by now.

It had to end in tears. Somewhere between getting off the dinghy and scrabbling over the seaweed Freya's shoes had got wet and it was *definitely* her brother's fault. A thin wailing rose from behind the rocky outcrop, the signal for father finally to row across and rescue Freya from the callous indifference of her feckless brother. Her shoes were wet and could he care? No of course he couldn't. 'But she slipped,' cried Ally, unconvincingly. Boys don't understand things like wet shoes and how traumatic that can be.

She got over her wet shoes soon enough, and even now is probably plotting revenge on her brother.

Wet, wet, wet

It's not easy to admit you've been a prat, but I've had some practice over the years. The other day I dropped in to see a boatbuilder of my acquaintance, Tim Loftus, late of Ullapool, now building an Ed Burnett 34-footer (10.3m) down in Cockenzie, near Edinburgh. Actually, building is too pedestrian a word. She's been crafted with extraordinary attention to detail: bronze floors, laminated beams, handmade fittings, and so on. 'Come up,' says Tim. So I nip smartly up the ladder and gaze around me in awe. I'm transfixed – not a bad word as it happens.

'No, wet, wet,' says Tim. What's he on about? Oh bugger. The deck paint's still wet.

I unstick my shoes, leaving behind a muddy tread mark, and step up onto the teak lazarette hatch cover. Bugger. I'm stuck to the hatch this time, with paint. So I spring lightly down into the cockpit (it's also wet). Then up again onto the teak cockpit seats (see above). Finally, under the pitying gaze of Tim and his father (who's handiwork I have ruined) I tear off my shoes and chuck them over the side. I'd not have been surprised to hear a yell of fury from the yard foreman passing below with a gallon of hot bitumen.

Having dabbled in the occult, and made a fool of myself generally, it's back this month to the real world, and the gales that have been blowing without a break since mid-November up here in Wester Ross. One after another, nasty little secondary depressions have been spinning off at high speed towards Loggie Bay where *Sally* is moored to a new length of $5/8$ in chain clove hitched and shackled to a hefty piece of ground tackle attached to two large anchors. It's not nearly hefty enough, however, to give me peaceful nights.

One night last week, our croft house was literally shaking to its foundations and the chickens, if they had not been bedded down safely in their wooden bunker, would have been flying horizontally past our bedroom. Next morning whirligigs of spume were being lifted off the wave tops and a big ferro cement ketch was up on the beach. *Sally* was riding safely to her mooring, sheltered by the hills, the wind broken by the birch and alder that fringe the little rocky bay.

And by heck, it's been wet. The river burst its banks, the fields are running with water and skeins of wind-blown spray are driving right to left down the valley as I write. There's a trio of sheep marooned on an island, my boat shed's leaking from a skylight and the drain's blocked. This is no weather to be working outdoors; this is weather to curl up by the wood burner with a book.

As for *Sally*? What more can I do. Ah, you say, there's always the insurance. And yet somehow that doesn't seem right; to profit from the loss of a boat that's survived since 1937. Which is why, this year, for the first time, I made the decision not to insure her. Foolish? Maybe. If ever she is lost, then I'll be inconsolable; no amount of money could make amends. Meantime I'll continue to check the shackles and renew the chafing pads and, like all owners of boats on swinging moorings, when the wild winds of winter blow, pray she stays safe.

Ssshailing (hic)

Soft! I can hear the whump of angry mailbag on editor's desk. Tread carefully Morgan, whispers a wee voice in my ear, for you venture on perilous waters. Here goes. The other day, a rare and blessed day of brilliant Hebridean sunshine, on calm seas, when fluffy clouds barely smudged an otherwise clear blue sky, and a gentle southerly riffled the surface of Annat Bay, you would have found me at the helm of my little wooden boat, humming along to a Mozart opera, glass in hand and, quite frankly, three sheets to the wind.

I'm not talking paralytic, just gently pissed. The kind of effect that half a bottle of red has of a hot, lazy summer afternoon on a contented mind, in a small classic wooden boat, when all seems, fleetingly, right with the world.

It was, I realise, shocking behaviour, unseamanlike; on The Solent my contentment might have been shattered at any moment by the wail of sirens and the flash of blue lights. Might even have been breathalised – and serve me right – supertankers, QE2, Cowes ferry, dozy yachtsman. Stupid.

But this was Annat Bay, and not another vessel of any description in sight. And as it was a Sunday (the Sabbath), the CalMac ferry was safely tied up in Stornoway. And no sign of any fishing boats either. Just me, on a 70-year-old boat I know like the back of my hand, listening to Mozart, arm draped lazily over tiller.

So why is it that we can confess to every sin in the book – grounding on a falling tide, mucking up our pilotage, falling overboard, adding our declination rather than subtracting – and yet no one, but no one (and I've read a thousand yachting stories) has ever confessed to being gloriously, happily and, I would argue, innocuously and gently tipsy in charge of a small yacht on a sunny day?

Strange that. When one recalls that Britain's maritime greatness was based on the courage of her jack tars, bolstered by liberal doses of rum. Or that solo sailors from Marin-Marie to Chichester and Knox-Johnston have enjoyed a sundowner. And that for many South Coast yachtsmen the primary reason for owning a boat is so they can nip across the Channel to hoover up crateloads of cheap booze.

So what is the harm in drifting about on the fringes of the Minch, on a clear day with a glass in hand and a broad grin on one's face? Days like that Sunday are rare enough up here. It's mostly oilskins and thick mitten weather, even in midsummer. A day such as that is to be savoured, I was about to say like good wine, until I remembered that it was a drop of cheapish plonk that had provided the beatific grin.

But believe me, it happens so rarely. I learnt my lesson long ago sailing back up The Hamble, alone, when tiller lashed, I so nearly piled *Sally* into a Sigma 33 lying to a fore-and-aft mooring near Mercury. Only takes a small beer to cloud your judgement.

And, honest, it probably won't happen again. Not, that is, until Hell freezes over or the next day dawns when I can sail in shirtsleeves on the Minch (whichever comes sooner).

Just had to get it off my chest, for my sake and for all those who may, once or twice – not regularly, you understand – just may have taken a wee dram while sailing a little boat they know well, in perfect contentment, under a clear blue sky on a glassy sea, and not another boat in sight. For that we should surely make no apologies.

Sublime or ridiculous?

What does a William Fife-designed Edwardian racing yacht have in common with a Ness sgoth (that's a Hebridean dipping lug-sailed 33ft (10m) clinker fishing boat from the last century)?

Answer: they are both very quick, if only for different reasons. The Fife was swift because she was a racing boat – pointless in itself – built in order to carry off some ornate Edwardian silverware, polish the owner's ego and make a bob or two in side bets (the crew had a stake in winning too, of course). The sgoth was quick for an altogether less frivolous reason: to carry back another flashy bounty – the silver darlings, the herring that once abounded and which fed the bellies of the poor and the poor fishermen who chased them in all weathers.

So, you might well ask, what would have more reason to be quick? Which is the more refined shape? The lean, long, lovingly varnished Fife or the rude-looking fishing boat with her huge beam, flared bow and brutally simple rig?

With a cup at stake and the sniff of prize money, the crew of a racing yacht would expect to go give it their all for honour, pride and a share of the winnings. Yet no large racing yacht's prize money more than scratched the cost of her building. On the other hand the sgoth would need to have paid her way, and paid her building costs in the first or second season at the fishing. That meant her crew had greater incentive to fine tune her; to get her to the fishing grounds and back efficiently. Her sails would have set to perfection. Their families livelihoods depended on a fresh catch delivered fast, and the men's lives on the strength of their sgoth, caught out in a winter gale off the Butt of Lewis.

This may sound obvious, but it came to me afresh in a blinding flash. In July I was aboard the Fife *Moonbeam* on the Clyde, and last month we sailed across the North Minch from Ullapool to Stornoway in *Sally* for the Hebrides Maritime Festival (which, if I forget to tell you is the best, friendliest and cheapest regatta we've attended). One evening, as we sat on Topher Dawson's classic plywood trimaran (30 years old), Kenny Morrison, *An Sulaire's* skipper, swung past, dipped his lug and invited us aboard.

'Oh well,' I thought. 'A sedate turn around the harbour before supper wouldn't go amiss.' For I had the impression that the sgoth *An Sulaire* was a clumsy sort of craft as finely tuned as a pub piano.

Ha! Take it from me: she's a racing boat, as slippery and responsive as any I have sailed. The dipping lug, far from being crude is a most wondrous invention. So it takes six fit men about 30 seconds to tack (14 is the record), but what efficiency: no stays (the main halyard doubles as a shroud) and no windage apart from that stout stump of pine, no boom to smack you over the head and almost infinite ways to set, reef and tune the sail.

The shore was soon hissing by, so fast yet so quietly that I had to look over the stern. *An Sulaire* hardly troubles the water with her passing. The wake was flat smooth, the tiller vibrating in my hand told the tale. We were on the wind and doing perhaps seven knots in a light evening breeze from the east. Then, to show off, Kenny short tacked her around the inner harbour. A Lewis man was heard to say '*An Sulaire*, why she's the best boat in all the islands.'

Earlier that month she had indeed been caught out off the Butt of Lewis. And while the waves were meeting in sheer jumps, *An Sulaire* stayed dry and safe. And when it came time to free off, she surfed downwind, the air sucking up into her lands providing lift and buoyancy. So which was the finer designer: old Fife or the anonymous fishermen who, over the centuries, refined that sgoth?

Highland yacht maintenance

To the Summer Isles and possibly beyond this summer, Rona and I, *Sally* the white boat, and Bran the chocolate-coloured pointer puppy will go. We'll drop a hook off Tanera Mhor, and set sail for lands where darkness never falls. We'll go a-Viking (without as much pillage and rape).

With all that scraping, painting, varnishing and engineering we habitually do it's as well to remind ourselves why we do it. To go places. Personally I'm as happy working on a boat as sailing her, and I'm sure that many people secretly agree. Which is why working and sailing *Sally* have become synonymous. We return from places in better shape than when we left. And I'm not talking spit and polish.

When we wooden boat nuts talk about work, it's the real thing. Burning off layers of enamel down to pitch pine topsides; scarphing in a new section of toe rail and re-hanging the rudder. Not polishing – oh for heaven's sake – the stainless steel stanchions. And with a special stainless steel stanchion polish. I ask you.

Now I'm going to permit myself to have a wee go at glassfibre and modern boats in general. Hitherto I have tended to ignore them, as if 50

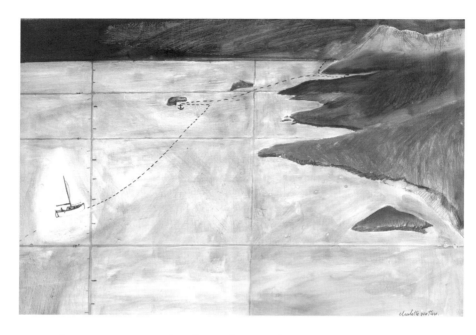

years of progress never existed. Truth is, underneath my classic, weather-beaten, besmocked, pipe-smoking, scruffy exterior I'm a qualified fan of fibres. Only last week we swanned around the Caribbean in a Jeanneau 43 and very nice it was too. No soul or character of course, and yet it served. Nothing much in the way of maintenance. Except perhaps the brightwork.

For brightwork on a glass boat read stainless steel, acrylic and plastic. When next you set foot in the chandlery take a look at the polish section. Now there's a potion to remove tar stains from fenders, scratches from hatches and any number that will guarantee to bleach out the rust marks left by the anchor chain on your foredeck. But the one I once saw that woman in Mercury Marina cleaning her stanchions with takes the biscuit.

Recently I counted 37 different kinds of polish in one yachting magazine, at around £10.99 a squeeze. Now tell me, honestly, which of you classic boat owners last bought any of them? Go on, feel smug. I do. If there's a rusty chain mark on my foredeck I leave it a season or two, then when next it's time to paint the deck, I paint out the stain. *Sally's* like the Forth Rail Bridge; and thank goodness, for what else would I do in harbour or at anchor when everyone else is lounging about sipping cocktails? (Or polishing their stanchions).

So cruising for me is more like extended maintenance. The log for July 2003, therefore, reads:

'Sunday, anchored Loch Goil. Stripped cockpit and varnished. Showers. Varnish ruined. Monday am, en route to Ardrishaig. No wind. Replaced engine oil. Violent squalls. Cleaned bilge of spilt engine oil,' etc.

Those little anchor symbols on charts remind me not so much of raptured nights under the starry panoply as of chores completed. Which rather connects my kind of sailing with my forefathers'. I'm thinking still of the Caribbean here, as in Western Careenage, on Mayreau, where they hauled down the ships to burn off the growth and lay on the pitch, Hurricane Hole and Polish the Pinnace Bay (OK, I made that up). 'Stanchion Buff Creek' doesn't have nearly the same ring to it.

Swimming? No fear

The observant among you – which means all but the skinny bloke in faded oilskins perched on the bridgedeck, with a cup of cocoa, fag on, blocking the companionway (don't you just hate it when they do that?) – will have noticed the deliberate mistake here. Picture of a boat and a girl swimming. In Loch Broom? You gotta be joking. She'd be as blue as that antifouling by the time the Sea King plucked her to safety and whisked her off to hospital in Inverness.

Now I am being unfair, in that the weather up here when it's good (like the little boy) is very very good. And when it's bad it's horrible, nasty, vicious, cold, wet and one day it wouldn't surprise me to find frogs raining from the sky (no chance of locusts, too cold and nothing, not even a hungry midge, can beat upwind against a Hebridean sou'wester).

But heyho. Artists are artists, and Charlotte (for it is she who drew the picture) is young and optimistic. Must be, as she and her partner Dan have embarked on a lengthy restoration of a 1920s cruising yacht with the usual problems.

The explanation as to why she chose to illustrate this drivel with a picture like that may have been in order to propitiate the gods. For Charlotte is embarking on a trip north, to the far north in fact, with a septuagenarian adventuress on board a little boat for a few months. Before she went she handed me a sheaf of illustrations with a 'Here, write something around those for a change'. It was challenge I could not resist. As an attempt to placate the north winds, I hope it works.

But I can tell you now that no one would go swimming in the loch, even in midsummer. The Gulf Stream, which is supposed to bathe these shores, takes a loop offshore at Rhuba Reidh – the big headland to the south of us (you know, the one with the Admiralty warning 'here be dragons') – and heads off towards Cape Wrath, where it swings right en route for Sweden. But again, I have my doubts about that. A warm current that starts in the Gulf of Mexico ends up warming the skerries off Gothenburg? Pull the other one.

Spring came late to Loch Broom (Gulf Stream or no) and it was mid-May when the boats were finally launched from their collection of gimcrack trailers, down the stony beach in front of the sailing club. All went well, apart from one sorry episode in which I played a key role. The little Blackwater Sloop I refurbished some years back has two sizeable holes punched in her quarters from ill-fitting trailer pads. Why? Impatience. Instead of waiting for the next tide my owner (why, oh why did I not positively insist he waited rather than just say 'be it one your own head'?) opted to go for it. Result? Two cracked planks and lots of scraped paint. Not terminal (nothing is on an old boat) but I could have done without the work.

Hell. Given the slim chance of good weather up here, I want to get out on the water, take *Sally* to the Outer Isles, lap up the sunshine in that little anchorage on the inappropriately-named Summer Isles, go swimming (not). Don't want to be messing about with old boats with cracked frames.

5

Of Beards, Boats and Admiral Beaufort

Blowing up *Britannia*

I have three half models to my name; all by Peter Ward of Poole. The first is of *Sally*, of which you've probably heard enough (Vertue No2, love of my life, etc). The second is of the yacht *America*, the low black schooner which, in 1851, took the cream of the British yachting fleet to the cleaners or, if you like revisionist history, was a *slow*, black schooner which just happened to meet the cream of the British fleet on a bad day. And she went the wrong side of a mark to boot. Again, enough said.

The third, and probably my favourite, is of the King's yacht *Britannia*; or kings', the kings being Edward VII and his son George V, both of whom loved her in a way that any wooden boat owner will understand. In 635 races she won 231 firsts out of a total of 360 prizes – a record that is unlikely ever to be equalled, let alone bettered.

'*Britty*' was a prodigious creation, measuring 121ft 6in (37m) overall on a waterline of 87ft 9in (26.8m). With a beam of 23ft 4in (7.1m), she drew just over 15ft (4.6m), and displaced 154 tons. Under her original gaff rig she spread 10,000 sqft (931sqm) of canvas. The base of her sail plan from tip of bowsprit to end of boom was 172ft (52.4m). With her 3-ton Oregon pine lower mast measuring 80ft (24.4m) and her topmast 58ft (17.7m), her sail plan towered over 142ft (43.2m) above deck.

George Watson designed her and Henderson's on the Clyde built her. 'So proud,' wrote James Meikle, a yachting correspondent, 'over her building were the men that the putting of her together was a real labour of love. Really it was not difficult to imagine that the framework was woven together, so beautifully were the many parts joined in to and on to each other.'

Composite built of wood planking over steel frames, she had been refitted extensively in 1935, at her end (she was scuttled off St Catherine's light) her Lloyds classification would have been current until 1940.

My modest part in her story is simply that, one fine day in April 1983 found me in the Public Records office in Kew, enquiring after the logbooks of HM destroyers *Amazon* and *Winchester*, the luckless pair that were detailed to preside over her scuttling.

After a lengthy wait, a box emerged from the vaults, containing the documents that were to form the core of an article I was preparing on the anniversary of her building. *Winchester's* log, unopened until that day, was typically to the point. It reads: '0245 slipped and sank *Britannia* in position Lat 50 34 18 N, Long 110 W.' It was only later, following a tip-off from an old colleague, Bill Beavis, that I chanced upon the one living eyewitness of the event.

Able Seaman Torpedoman Cyril 'Bods' Bodsworth, as his naval chums called him, was 19 years old, the youngest member of *Winchester's* crew.

He was 76, by the time I spoke to him, and living quietly in retirement near Portsmouth with his memories and a single memento of the night when he blew *Britannia*'s bilges and deckhead apart with four carefully prepared gun cotton charges.

All did not go according to plan, that July night in 1935, he told me. The charges failed to blow. 'Those who had made them were beginning to sweat. We thought "Oh dear we are going to be in dead trouble". Luckily someone must have opened the seacocks,' Bods recalled. 'After about a quarter of an hour we heard just a gentle pop.

'A bit later we heard this much larger explosion, and one solitary deck plank shot up out of the water and did a gentle parabola in the light of our searchlight. We spent the rest of night looking for the wreckage. We never found that plank.'

Bods did not go home completely empty handed, however, from his night's work. 'In spite of what we had been told about no souvenirs, there was this cocktail cabinet, wooden Victorian-style furniture, with wooden spikes to keep in the bottles,' he remembered. 'One of them was a bit loose, and just fitted my rule pocket. It's in my attic. No one can prove where it came from but I know it came from the *Britannia*.'

Now that, not the dry conservation or the patient recreation of an old boat, is history. For without people, boats are just artefacts.

Kiss me Hardy

Dark and windy night in our Highland crofthouse, no telly, read everything, so we had the Ouija board out. It took me a moment to twig that I'd picked up Horatio Nelson, and it came as quite a shock, especially as I'd asked to be put through either to Horace, a forebear on my mother's side who was purported to have stashed away a fortune in Kruger rands before passing away while fishing the Test last August, or failing that another relative, Horatio Sprague, US consul in Gibraltar when they towed in the *Mary Celeste*. No matter; what did England's most celebrated admiral want, I wondered?

'Need to set a few things straight, young man.'

Bee in his cocked hat about yachtsman's ignorance of flag etiquette maybe? Something trivial from the great man. That's often the way.

'Bout time we buried this Trafalgar nonsense once and for all. What's it bin? Two hundred years? Bless me soul. Can't ye leave me old bones in peace?'

Things were looking up. I grabbed my notebook. 'But we do it to honour your memory, our hero.'

'Well don't. And that popinjay who prances around impersonating me with *that woman* on his arm, 'strewth, they trouble me sorely. My Emma was, bless me soul, a deuced sight more generously endowed than that slip of a girl. No tumblehome to speak of. Careening her'd be like heaving down a pinnace. My Emma was a first rate. Ship o' the line. Broad in the beam, well fastened. When I came alongside, threw the grapples and fired me opening broadside...'

He carried on it that vein for some time, speaking of buttock lines and stays – you can probably imagine – until I was forced to interrupt him, and advise that we lived in less exuberant times, and besides, my editor was a Quaker. I lied. He sighed.

'Pish. Where was I?'

'Trafalgar?'

'Ah yes. Trafalgar. Struck down in the thick of the fighting. But then it was my ticket to immortality and a prime spot in St Paul's, though I'd have preferred a more weatherly gauge.'

'So the sparkly medals and the full uniform on the poop deck was on purpose, to attract attention?'

'Nonsense. Remember when I left Portsmouth? Dashing down the steps to me cutter in full kit? Gets on board the old *Vicky*, stows me gear and – low and behold – seems Emma's forgotten to pack me second best. She's

not only forgot me brown trousers, me smalls, me cravats, me silk stockings, but she's sent me off with some of her stuff. So there I am, off to fight the Frenchies with seventy-two pairs of camisole knickers, a t'gallant's-worth of lace petticoats, fourteen bodices and seven ostrich feather bonnets. Typical of the woman. Body like a goddess, brain like a colander.'

'So it was either the full dress, or Emma's underwear, your lordship?'

'Exactly. Kept that stuff for the privacy of me own cabin. Nothing like a freshly laundered pair of Emma's knickers on a long passage. Remember we chased them Frenchies from Ushant to the Indies and back before we cornered them off Trafalgar. Clean underwear twice a week. Splendid.'

'And that "Kiss me Hardy" stuff?'

'Pah. Delirium. I was fast fading and here's this vision of sobbing loveliness in lace bending over me, bodice heaving. It was my Emma! Here at my last! Bliss! So, yes; I did say "Kiss me" and "Hardy", but it wasn't like that.

'When I saw Emma me heart leapt. "Kiss me", I croaked. Then a pause as the mist cleared and there was me old whiskery mate, flag captain Hardy, inches from me face, ear cocked for me last words, not the blessed Emma after all. "… Hardy?!!!", I said, with some measure of surprise. Too late. Ah well. It beats that fellow whose last words were something about bringing him one of Bellamy's meat pies, though I wished I'd thought of "I think I can smell burning". Brilliant, quite brilliant, don't yer think, young man?'

Gale? What gale?

The old boat is in my mind almost constantly now, waking and sleeping. Down south the gales are blowing and a storm is curling in from the Atlantic. Worrying times. The newspapers – with no thought to the feelings of those whose boats are lying to moorings 500 miles away – are calling it 'the perfect storm' as if that would make things better. 'She sank in the perfect storm,' you'd say. Thanks a bunch.

More likely – and my fingers are crossed – it'll be about as perfect as everything else the papers say about the weather, with scant regard for accuracy or history or Sir Francis Beaufort, the longest serving hydrographer to the navy and the man who, when all's said and done, invented the wind.

He'd be turning in his lead-lined casket, letting out the most explosive harrumphs, 'by my souls' and 'I beg your pardons'.

How often do you read of some unfortunate angler caught out in a 'force 5 gale'? How often do you hear of a storm when they mean a gale? And when exactly does a gale become a storm to the headline writers anyway? Answer: when the word fits the headline space available on the page. Poor old Francis Beaufort. All those years of observation; all those scratchy quill pens broken in search of the *bon mot* to accurately describe a force 10. Scratch, scratch: should it be spume blown in creamy streaks, or streaky foam? Too theatrical. Scratch, scratch: what does the wind sound like? Moaning like a woman in ecstasy? Ahem, I think not. How about 'quite noisy, or reasonably noisy?' Scratch, scratch: and would the sea be roiling, boiling or tumbling. When precisely does spindrift become spume?

Best, thought Beaufort, to keep it understated, like the RNLI reports of rescues. 'Cox'n Bill Boggins was fortunate that the second wave did not carry the Devonforth lifeboat *Mabel Gracey* onto The Jags, by now no more than 1 cable to leeward. The wind was probably gusting hurricane force 12, as the anemometer needle was hard against its stops, and only skilful throttle control allowed Boggins to judge the set of the waves and back his lifeboat onto the deck of the freighter, which he did seven times before all the crew were accounted for…' You've read them, I'm sure.

Beaufort could so easily have gone over the top, like we all do after the second double at the yacht club bar. Morgan's Scale would then read something like this: 'Force 10. Absolute hell on water. Totally wild, with enormous bloody waves. Wind noise like a shrieking banshee, can't see a blind thing. Liferaft on deck. We're all doomed', etc. 'Force 12: Nothing for it but to pray. Crew will be a gibbering wreck. Don't even think of going on deck. Sea like a boiling maelstrom. Nothing can live in this? Surely. Oh God, we are all going to die'.

But no, after the bit about tumbling wave crests Francis Beaufort ends with something alike 'Visibility seriously affected…'. Now that's stiff upper lip. Something which Our Island Media seem to have mislaid when addressing Our Island Race. We can forgive them the High Tide bit as in 'The town of Shrewsbridge is bracing itself for the next onslaught when the river Shrew is expected to reach danger levels at 4am, the next High Tide.' High Water we all get wrong, despite the old adage and convenient aide memoire about Come Hell or High Water. Come Hell or High Tide doesn't have the same ring.

This sloppy use of words to describe the ebb and flow that dictates our life is the most obvious example of how we have lost touch with the sea. The natural world of floods and disasters is filtered through the uncomprehending filter of the weather presenter and her 'it's going to be a ber-right and a ber-reezy day for everyone in the south, with windy weather over exposed coastlines'.

Which makes the old BBC Shipping Bulletins such an invaluable touchstone in a world when a gale is anything from force 5 and a storm begins as soon as you need it to make a headline.

The Ranting Fifties

I still shudder at the memory; the time I left muddy boot prints on my friend Tim Loftus's newly painted deck. To make me feel less of a heel (ha!) he told me about Olin Stephens catching a splinter and bleeding all over the bare woodwork of a new boat he'd designed. The owner simply encapsulated the great man's stigmata under six coats of varnish, forever. Can't imagine my boot mark survived much past Tim's first expletive.

On the embarrassment scale it cannot compare to the time we charged into Cowes under full canvas and missed T-boning a Daring by a weasel's whisker, or blocked the Wareham Channel on a Bank Holiday Monday, causing a cursing tailback as far as Round Island. Yes, of cock-ups (as Sinatra might have sung) I've had my share.

Mention of Sinatra reminds me of my age. Is it automatic that after 50 we start to get cranky? Wear blue serge yachtsman's caps, covered in badges, and sport red ochre trousers? Grow a beard? Delight in obscure nautical phraseology, or insist on correct flag etiquette? Do 'classic yachtsmen' need to affect a uniform, dress down? Must we all hold opinions about glassfibre that, if applied to foreigners would be called racist, and generally complain that 'things ain't what they used to be'?

It's refreshing to see classic boats owned by the under 30s, not always the over 50s, with their predictable views on the other man's plastic boat. I've been guilty myself, denigrating everything from plywood and epoxy to what I see as ugly boats. My opinions come back to haunt me from time to time, and I have to remind myself to keep an open mind as the years roll by, admit that flying from a trapeze in a carbon fibre sports boat might just be more exciting than trundling along at 5 knots in a 70-year-old Vertue.

Reading the reports from the Volvo Round the World Race is a case in point. Despite keels failing and bulkheads cracking there's no denying it sounds fun, racing on the edge of control, bouncing off sunken containers and skimming icebergs. However, I did baulk some weeks back at the skipper of one of the yachts which hit and killed a shark. 'Exciting,' he called it. At which I thought: 'What, bludgeoning an animal to death with a lump of lead? Surely not'.

Are we so drunk on speed and adrenaline that we've forgotten our respect for a poor old shark going about its business? So I emailed a friend, a veteran of several round the world races, America's and Admiral's Cups. The oceans of the world to him were magical places. Racing yachtsmen were in danger of forgetting what a privilege they now enjoy.

'.... they have drifted apart from reality and could be described as unhuman, doing something that few other people could or would do,' he wrote in reply. '... in the process their flotsam of feelings seems caught up on the hanging branches of commerce. The oceans are an intoxicating place for us humans to float over... what a unique feeling and privilege, that mere humans at a basic level, can endure the passage of the wind, waves and currents of an ancient leviathan.'

Has a way with words our Craig. But then, having spent half a lifetime screaming around the world on Kevlar ironing boards, he now sails a 71-year-old Harrison Butler with which he terrorises Sigmas and Moodys around The Solent. Kind of settles a man's mind owning an old wooden boat. Not one of your flimsy plastic jobs (Heck. Here I go again...)

Dang

Why ain't mo' people heard o' Robb White? Boatbuilder? Ya have? Better ship off ter the nex' page. Dang (as Robb would say).

To those who ain't (I should say haven't) heard of Mr White, he was also a writer and sage from Thomasville, Georgia with quite a following 'cross the ol' pond. Heck, there I go again, that's what a week's holiday in Florida does to you. His boats are fast and light and his approach was unique. He wouldn't quote a price; wouldn't let you see the boat until it

was finished; wouldn't set a delivery date; most certainly wouldn't discuss any aspect of the boat with you while he was building her. May not even have parted with her. 'The whole business is my business, not their business,' he would say. There was a waiting list for his boats as long as the beach on Dog Island where he escaped every summer to test them.

As a writer, Robb provoked as much ire as admiration. He was, one might say, provocative. About boats, despoilers of nature, property developers and the purveyors of plywood ('the devil's work'). His chosen materials were tulip poplar and epoxy, heat cured in a unique process that produced extraordinarily light, elegant boats for which he became renowned. His Atkin-modified shoal draught planing boat Rescue Minor is a case in point. He was a wise and lucky man – owned 1,200 acres of virgin pine forest, including some of the only surviving long leaf yellow pine in the world.

What made Robb so interesting to a fellow boatbuilder (though I hesitate to bracket myself with him) were his methods. For a start he induced curves in $^1/_8$ in tulip poplar planking for his crazily lightweight boats under heat lamps (and a tin hat to protect his brain cells). Encapsulated in glass cloth and 'epoxified' it produced clinker dinghies far stronger than plywood. Lighter too. Much lighter. 'Don't give a fat rat's ass fo' plywood,' he would say.

I had the privilege of meeting Robb in his clearing in the woods outside Thomasville shortly before his death, where he lived with his wife and son (who's also a boatbuilder) and a collection of most unusual boats, cars, engines and such. He took us to see his long leaf pine, a material of which I am inordinately fond as my old Vertue is planked in the stuff.

Increasingly, however, after a lifetime studying marine life forms, driving tugs up mangrove rivers on Florida's Gulf Coast (he'd tell you he was just the cook) and building small boats, in his latter years he wrote – in particular a column in the bi-monthly *Messing About In Boats*. *How to Build a Tin Canoe* is the autobiography of a wild Georgia boy, of boats and fishing and all kinds of quirky, unrelated stuff in which his voice comes through as clear as a whippoorwill.

Among his stories (and to be honest they lose a deal in translation) comes one about the new boat he was trialling near his family's beach house on Dog Island – a near-deserted stretch of old Florida barrier island off Apalachicola Bay – he chances upon what he reckons is a dead turtle, which he circles and hauls aboard. Turns out it's not dead, and then it eats his new boat. It's the kind of story you don't hear on this side of the great divide.

More's the pity, for voices like Robb's are rare indeed. But enough of me: catch yourself a copy of *How to Build a Tin Canoe*. Better hurry, like his boats, 'fore long it'll just be a collector's item. Dang.

JDS remembered

Des Sleightholme will be remembered for many things: his long editorship of *Yachting Monthly*, his Old Harry stories, his sea sense and wisdom and for the stories he told about himself; well, against himself would be more accurate, for he was pretty self-effacing. They would often as not involve 'Sleightholme's luck', which was legendarily bad. If there were clear skies over Walton Backwaters, his favourite East Coast haunt, there'd be a black cloud and hailstones over Des's chosen corner of it.

In particular it was his luck never to have the boat he properly deserved. As editor of *Yachting Monthly* for 18 years he could have had the pick of the boat shows. Instead he made do for many years with *Tinker Liz*, a 24ft (7.3m) sloop that became so idiosyncratic under his ownership it was a miracle she ever found a buyer when eventually Des decided it was time to move up to something even more cranky and inappropriate.

I'd have loved to have been around at *Tinker Liz's* handing over.

Des: 'Now this bungee cord holds this flap. Pull out this pin and this piece of plywood hinges up automatically to give you extra chart space. Simple,' (pause to show how it worked) then Twaaang, 'Oh bugger...'

The same went for the bunks and the galley work surface, the echo sounder bracket ... In retrospect, *Tinker Liz* can be seen for what she was: an early prototype for those transformer toys – press this button and the

BMW Series 3 turns into the Flesh Eating Intergalactic Scorpion. Except that, for all the turn-buttons and bungee, *Tinker Liz* remained 24ft (7.3m) long. Inside, however, she was a B&Q Tardis.

Des will be remembered best, though unfairly, for creating Old Harry, a comic character that many readers confused for its author and from whom Des unsuccessfully tried to distance himself. His inept creation dogged him like an embarrassing uncle; the one with the flashing bowtie and a penchant for risky jokes at inappropriate times. In truth he bore some resemblance to the old codger, even he would not deny it.

My favourite memory of Des dates back to the days when I worked on *Yachting Monthly*. Every month we had to dream up a practical exercise for the edification of what Des – a newspaperman before he became a yachting editor – called 'dear reader'. One month we'd be making danbuoys out of fenders, telescopic fishing rods, duck tape, hand torches and condoms (to keep the light watertight), the next doing blind navigation exercises. This month Des had it in mind to investigate the carrying power of the human voice. Just how far could you be heard downwind or upwind? Would intonation aid understanding? Or pitch and pronunciation?

Now this would be useful stuff in an emergency. No point dear reader, yacht drifting, blood gushing from a head wound hailing a passing yacht 'Fetch me a doctor, quick' if it came over as 'Get me a locksmith'. *YM* had a duty to enlighten. No expense or embarrassment would be spared. So we devised a test, off Walton Backwaters (of course). Des was to row off downwind with a prepared script which I was to note down as I heard it.

What they made of the respected editor of their favourite magazine standing in a dinghy yelling in falsetto, 'I have a sick monkey on board, do you have a doctor?' I cannot imagine. Actually it was 'I-a-a-ik-unkey-o-bore. Do-oo-a-a-ocker?' as Des had this sneaking suspicion that sound carried further if you left out some of the consonants, oh and enunciated the phrase in a high pitched voice.

The old salts are slipping their moorings, gone to Fiddler's Green, or some nautical equivalent of shuffling off mortal coils. Des would probably call it 'falling off his perch'. Then he'd light his pipe and chuckle.

Shared heritage

Let's be serious for a change. I'm tempted to get shot of my entire library. Sailing is not exactly a world shatteringly important enough subject to have 40 yards of bookshelf devoted to it.

I have always thought that we who write about boats belong to a very insignificant band. It's a topic that does not alter lives in any major way.

We cover a pastime that is pleasurable, but essentially frivolous; this is not, to use a cliché, brain surgery.

Nor is sailing held in any great esteem by what a Victorian yachtsman might have called 'the great unwashed', or for that matter by today's red top sports editors. Hell, can you imagine anyone saying of a yacht race: 'It isn't a matter of life and death, it's more important than that'. Unless some poor bloke's keel falls off in the Southern Ocean. We know better than to inflate our pastime from the sublime into the ridiculous.

Face it: by and large the story of yachting is populated by chinless toffs, the idle rich and brave idiots such as Lord Cardigan who lived aboard his yacht during the Crimean War and led the light cavalry into the Valley of Death. We have less to be guilty of today, perhaps, and the demographics of yachting are arguably broader than they have ever been, and yet it's still not a very inclusive pursuit. Even to design yachts cannot compare to designing passenger liners, ferries, warships or bulk carriers. Yacht cruising is A Trivial Pursuit.

Nevertheless, Nelson also cruised in the *Victory*. He cruised to the West Indies to seek out Villeneuve, and cruised back again to bring the combined fleet to battle off Cape Trafalgar. Admirals Jellicoe and Beatty cruised from Scapa Flow and the Firth of Forth the length of the North Sea to shadow the German High Seas Fleet during the Great War. Beatty commanded a fleet of battle 'cruisers' and his superior officer, Jellicoe, Admiral of the Grand Fleet, had a whole range of cruisers at his disposal – armoured cruisers, light cruisers, etc. Thus the term cruising is common to both warriors and weekend cruising sailors.

And there's more to connect us cruising folk to a larger seafaring trad-ition. We navigate by the same lights and charts and use the same satellites as our professional counterparts. What's more, many of those who have commanded ships of war over the centuries have been small-boat sailors, from Second World War U-boat commander Herbert Werner to Admiral Woodward who led the fleet during the Falklands War (big change from his Sonata). Yachts had a huge influence on warship design in the early history of the Royal Navy, and those who paced quarter decks have often been as familiar with the cockpits of small racing yachts.

No, maybe yachting is not so frivolous. The man who can steer an ocean racer through a Fastnet storm surely makes for a more unflappable officer of the watch when the enemy fleet is sighted on the horizon. Waterloo may have been won on the playing fields of Eton, but it is arguable that Jutland was won (albeit debatably) on the waters of the Solent.

Which makes me feel rather less ashamed of what I do. It connects me directly to those who commandeered a flotilla of small craft and brought an army off the beaches of Dunkirk. And to the RNVR officers and men

who swept the minefields, and manned the small craft, MTBs and destroyers; even the battleships that sunk the *Bismarck* and the *Hood*, for that matter.

So why is it that little is written on yachting and the yachtsmen's vital role in times of war and national emergency? Now those would be books I'd be proud to keep in my collection, amid the ephemera and the trivia of a sport that is hardly a matter of life and death. Or is it?

Old men and the sea

If the sailing of small traditional craft is to prosper, and in order to encourage more youngsters and women to take an interest in classic dinghies, a major issue has to be addressed: beards.

You cannot fail to notice at classic boat gatherings and jumble sales the length of the land that the vast majority of those running their fingers over varnished gunwales or squinting at sheer lines or discussing the merits of standing over balanced lug rigs are men, usually over 50, and invariably bearded. Of women and the young there is usually no sign. And those that are present look impressed (in the sense they look as if they'd been rounded up by the Press Gang and shovelled into the family MPV).

There are exceptions: the other day I delivered a 15ft (4.6m) faering (yes, the one I've been wittering on about for months was finally delivered)

to a family in the Lake District. To a man, woman, boy and girl they were mad about little boats, and the children all wore red woolly hats like Swallows (or was it Amazons?). No sign of boredom there, and not a Game Boy to be seen anywhere. Heart warming.

Then along came the bearded ones. Now I have to be careful here as they are all good friends, who I respect and like a lot. And one of them was, to be honest, beardless. Oh, and there was also a young woman amongst them who would be sorely offended if I suggested she had even the slightest trace of a beard. Nevertheless, beardless or no, they all looked as if they *should* be bearded.

As a beardless one myself – any attempts have been pathetic – I am not a little envious of those old-fashioned, luxuriant chin bushes and side whiskers you still occasionally see. The ones that look as if they might shelter four larks and a wren or if shaken would disgorge the crumbs from half a loaf of wholemeal bread. These are seldom the beards one sees at British traditional boat gatherings, however, which are usually less flamboyant. More an excuse not to shave, or perhaps a disguise. Maybe even as a deterrent, for women, by and large, do not like straggly beards.

Little old boat gatherings are clearly among the last havens for the hunted and harassed and soon to be made redundant old British male; places where this endangered species can range around safely without dressing to attract a mate. He can poke about boat jumble with impunity, rummage through skeins of cheap rope, stroke varnish in peace, away from the critical gaze of spouse or partner, and converse endlessly about grommets, the genius of Albert Strange, centreboards and buttock lines without that tug on the sleeve that signifies 'I'm bored, I want to go home/get a burger/recharge my Game Boy/or sit in the car and watch telly'.

In America little old wooden boats are also largely owned, admired, stroked, varnished, built, designed and sailed by bearded men over the age of 50. However, the clothes are smarter, beards much neater – often modelled after Ernest Hemingway's. You will find throngs of Old Men of the Sea, lacking only a battered straw hat and a pair of ragged canvas trousers, and more women (anthropologists discuss).

Over here we need more young families in red woolly hats involved in little boats. And more women. Bottom line is: a bunch of bearded old geezers in scruffy jeans is not only unsightly but deeply unsexy. So smarten up lads.

Boatyard tyrants

Among the nuggets of advice I would hand down to any son the most important would be: 'nurture your boatyard owner'. Further than that, be downright ingratiating. Pay your bills by return and never, ever liberate a useful piece of teak from what looks like a pile of gash without offering the contents of the front pocket of your paint-stained overalls (having made sure you only carry a few coppers). Show willing, at least.

This is sound advice, believe me. Grumble about the cost of your berth, cavil at the extortionate hourly rate charged for plucking a tiny mast from a small boat and laying it on trestles, but do it in private, and pay up, on the button. You need him more than he needs you. And he knows it.

My first was formerly captain of one of Her Majesty's aircraft carriers. Having run a ship of a thousand souls and successfully launched a thousand aircraft, a few acres of propped up wood and glassfibre and a bunch of weekend boat owners was a piece of piss, as they say in the navy.

To a young owner he represented a terrifying prospect. I would steel myself before entering his office. No matter how much Miss Moneypenny who guarded this sanctum reassured me 'the boss is in a good mood today', it would evaporate when he saw me. No matter how carefully I coiled the yard hose, he'd make me feel as if I alone was responsible for lowering the tone of his entire establishment. 'Suppose you want to borrow something,' he'd predict, fairly accurately. 'Don't suppose you've come to pay your bill.' And even if I had come to fork out the ludicrous fee he charged to keep my tiny vessel in his muddy lagoon, accessible only an hour either side of high water, it was all I could do to keep myself from doffing my cap in gratitude.

I would fantasise a conversation beginning with 'Now look here...' and ending with '...in conclusion I have decided to take my custom elsewhere', except I knew he'd fall about: '...they're queuing up to take your berth. Might smarten the place up a bit, having shot of that ghastly excuse for a yacht you park in my marina.'

At least I left a parting eyesore when finally I plucked up the courage to leave his fiefdom. A rusting, useless road trailer.

Marinas offer plenty of scope for the impecunious wooden boat owner to fall foul of the apparatchiks running them. Dismantle the Baby Blake on their decking and hear the whir of the closed circuit TV camera zooming in. This happened at Puerto Banus in Spain where, in those days, you could find a poodle parlour and manicurist but nothing resembling a marine engineer, so what was a poor crew to do when the blasted thing got blocked up?

In writing this I run enormous risk. Yard proprietors are like old-fashioned bank managers; word spreads. I remember trying to change my account once. After the small matter of a large overdraft and a nasty letter it was an early case of: 'I have determined to take my business elsewhere...' Trouble is Barclays needed a reference from my previous manager. Thus, no deal, certainly no credit card. So it was back to NatWest cap in hand.

It would have been the same if ever I had been foolish enough to exert my rights as a boat owner. Luckily, well before that, I had learnt lesson number one: button your lip, whatever you feel about the scandalous price you pay to keep your priceless piece of floating heritage in his rat infested marine scrap yard.

Not all yards are thus. I remember a winter spent at a model establishment, run with fanatical efficiency. May I please borrow a ladder (they were all painted orange with the yard name stencilled on them)? Or a power line (£5 a day, £50 deposit 'it's 'cos you blighters are always running off with them, that's why')? Cleared my tab daily and swept up the sawdust in the shed. Still got the impression that he thought his yard would be a darned sight better if there weren't so many damned boat owners cluttering it up.

I was a model customer. Until launching day. 'Would I move my boat, soon as possible.' Certainly, sir. You know the form: drop everything, drive down crack of dawn, slap of antifoul under the impatient stares of the men. 'Oh, and when she's in perhaps you'd scrub off that blue mess you've splattered all over my clean launching slip...' And, of course, I did. Word gets around.

And finally …

Having at various times in writing slagged off bearded types, plywood boats and boats that don't go to windward I reckon I've alienated most of those ever-hopeful few who flip the page with a sigh and a 'Wonder what the heck he'll be on about this time?'

Will it be the splendour of sailing the Hebrides in a 70-year-old Vertue, of sea eagle-haunted creeks where only the cry of the gulls and the bark of the seals can be heard against the ceaseless roar and slurp of the breakers, etc, etc. Nope. Been off this year for just one week; the rest of the time it's been dreadful. Down south maybe they've been complaining about the heat, but not up here.

Maybe some nonsense about Ouija boards and an other-worldly encounter with the ghost of Nelson? Not this column's finest hour, I admit, although my contention that Horatio wore his finest on the quarter deck that fateful day because Emma forgot to pack his seagoing gear (and thus became a target for that French sharpshooter) has been taken up and debated heatedly, I am told, by the Faculty of Nelsonian Studies at the University of West Creek Virginia (poor fools).

Or will it be some long-drawn-out boatbuilding saga with a twist in the tail? I've a wooden cold moulded Folkboat in the yard at present that should by rights have been burnt, and it's providing the raw material for many a long winter month, but I'll save that for later as I know there are

scores of recently trained shipwrights out there screaming at the editor 'You give that bloke far too much space to plug his business already, when we're out here starving.' Actually, to set the record straight, I reckon I've scared off most potential customers by my honest admission of human failures. Besides, who wants to shell out for a new boat, no matter how fine or exquisite, and find him or herself the subject of a facetious article?

Doesn't leave much. On faithful restoration: I reckon if only the smell of the old boat remains that's a restoration. On varnish? Take the surface down to bare wood and lay on two or three coats of Blakes Wood Seal. It may smell like an adolescent glue sniffer's dream, but my goodness it sticks. And then what? Slap on any number of coats of your favourite varnish (Blakes Favourite is my favourite, for what it's worth) although their Classic is, er... more classic.

Finally, on plywood/epoxy sailing dinghies I'll just say that they are, by and large, far too light, skittish and hugely wasteful of timber. Moreover the grain invariably looks shite and epoxy is the devil's brew. Why bother when it's cheaper and more satisfying (and a damn sight easier I maintain) to build in solid timber? And none of that soul destroying cleaning up and scraping off of epoxy dribbles.

My friend Mr Oughtred and other designers, I am sure, who have made wooden boatbuilding more accessible will upbraid me for this. Maybe, but no traditional boat revival can be based on plywood and epoxy alone, let alone any number of stunning strip planked canoes or flat-bottomed skiffs. Gotta be proper.